Little Red Book
of
Phrasal Verbs

By the same author

Little Red Book Series

Little Red Book of Slang-Chat Room Slang	Little Red Book of Modern Writing Skills
Little Red Book of English Vocabulary Today	Little Red Book of Punctuation
Little Red Book of Grammar Made Easy	Little Red Book of Synonyms
	Little Red Book of Antonyms
Little Red Book of English Proverbs	Little Red Book of Common Errors
Little Red Book of Prepositions	Little Red Book of Letter Writing
Little Red Book of Idioms and Phrases	Little Red Book of Essay Writing
	Little Red Book of Word Fact
Little Red Book of Effective Speaking Skills	Little Red Book of Spelling
	Little Red Book of Language Checklist
Little Red Book of Euphemisms	Little Red Book of Perfect Written English
Little Red Book of Word Power	

A2Z Book Series

A2Z Quiz Book	A2Z Book of Word Origins

Others

The Book of Fun Facts	The Book of Motivation
The Book of More Fun Facts	Read Write Right: Common Errors in English
The Book of Firsts and Lasts	The Students' Companion
The Book of Virtues	
World Facts Finder	

Little Red Book *of* Phrasal Verbs

Terry O'Brien

RUPA
PUBLICATIONS INDIA

Published by
Rupa Publications India Pvt. Ltd 2012
7/16, Ansari Road, Daryaganj
New Delhi 110002

Sales centres:

Allahabad Bengaluru Chennai
Hyderabad Jaipur Kathmandu
Kolkata Mumbai

Copyright © Terry O'Brien 2012

All rights reserved.
No part of this publication may be reproduced, transmitted,
or stored in a retrieval system, in any form or by any means, electronic,
mechanical, photocopying, recording or otherwise, without the prior
permission of the publisher.

ISBN: 978-81-291-1967-4

Third impression 2015

10 9 8 7 6 5 4 3

Terry O'Brien asserts the moral right to be
identified as the author of this work.

Typeset by Innovative Processors, New Delhi

Printed at Shree Maitrey Printech Pvt. Ltd., Noida

This book is sold subject to the condition that it shall not, by way of
trade or otherwise, be lent, resold, hired out, or otherwise circulated,
without the publisher's prior consent, in any form of binding or cover
other than that in which it is published.

*I dedicate this book to late Prof. A.P. O'Brien,
my father, friend, guide and mentor, who
inspired me to the canon of excellence:
re-imagining what's essential*

Phrasal Verbs

A

- **abide by** (*keep to, adhere to*) I expect him to abide by his decision to help us. She will abide by her promise.
- **act out** (*act in full, present in a theatrical way*) He acted out all that had happened to him. In group therapy, patients can act out their problems.
- **act** (up)**on** (*do something definite about*) You should act upon this letter at once, or it will be too late.
- **act up** (*a*) (*behave badly*) The children have been acting up all day, and I'm exhausted. (*b*) (*perform erratically*) My car has started acting up and badly needs servicing.
- **add in** (*insert*) Would you add in these items, please, in order to complete the list?
- **add on** (*add as an extra or extras*) Would you please add these names on (to your list)? Add the other items on at the bottom of the page.
- **add together** (*intensive of* add) He added the numbers together.
- **add up** (*a*) (*total*) These figures don't add up right. (*b*) (*make sense*) It all adds up, I can see now why he left so suddenly. Nothing he does seem to add up.
- **add up to** (*a*) (*amount to*) The money he spent added up to more than ₹ 1,000. (*b*) (*signify, indicate*) The evidence all adds up to a case of murder.
- **admit of** (*leave room for*) This work admits of no delay.
- **agree with** (*a*) (*have same opinion as*) I can't agree with you in this matter. (*b*) (*coincide with*) His explanation

agrees with the facts of the situation. (*c*) (*suit the health of*) The climate of southern India agrees with me. Rich food doesn't agree with her. (*d*) (*approve of*) I don't agree with people drinking brandy all day long. (*e*) (*of verb, adjective etc.*) A verb always agrees with its subject.
- **allow + particle** (*permit, with direction*) The doorman allowed the people in one by one. They allowed me out in order to make a telephone call. The doctor allows her up for two hours each day, because she has made such excellent progress.
- **allow for** (*account of, make concession for*) You should allow for his poor eyesight. The company will allow for extra expenditure next year. When making up this kind of material, you should allow for shrinkage (in the wash).
- **amble + particle** (*walk slowly and gently, with direction*) The cows ambled along, chewing gently. He ambled up to me and asked what time it was.
- **answer back** 1 (*reply insolently*) Don't answer back like that! The little boy answered back cheekily to his father. 2 (*reply insolently to*) The little boy answered his father back several times.
- **answer for** (*a*) (*be responsible for*) You must answer for any missing articles after the party. They have a lot to answer for and must have uneasy consciences. (*b*) (*guarantee*) I will answer for the truth of his statements. He can answer for his son's behaviour.
- **answer to** (*correspond to, be in accord with*) A man answering to the police description was arrested in London last night.
- **average out** (*reach an average*) His taxes should average out at about one quarter of his income.
- **average out at** (*be averaged at*) Their working hours average out at 40 per week. His weekly earnings average out at Rs 3500.

B

- **babble away** (*babble, chatter continuously*) The children sometimes babble away for hours. He babbled away about his problems.
- **babble on** (*continue babbling, unpleasantly*) She babbled on about her problems. He was babbling on about his golf score.
- **babble out** (*say or emit in a babble of words*) In his fear, he babbled out the names of his accomplices. She babbled out something I couldn't understand.
- **back away** 1 (*retreat*) The frightened horse backed away from the snake. 2 (*reverse away*) He backed the lorry away, so that we could get into the garage.
- **back down** (*a*) (*descend backwards*) He backed down carefully while I held the ladder for him. The car at the top of the slope backed slowly down. (*b*) (*give way, yield*) He backed down and accepted our proposals. The trade union expects the management to back down. They are too proud to back down and admit mistakes.
- **back on to** (*be neighbour to, at the back*) The house backs on to a market garden.
- **back up** 1 (*move up backwards*) The trucks backed up as fax as possible to make room for the others. 2 (*a*) (*move up backwards*) They backed the trucks up as much as possible, to make room for the others. (*b*) (*support*) I hope you will back me up in this argument. He always backs up his friends. Nobody backed her up when she protested against the decision. I'll back your story up, if they ask me about it.
- **bail out** (*a*) (*pay money as a surety for*) His brother bailed him out (of prison). He was bailed out. (*b*) (*help in an emergency*) I hope someone will bail me out of this.

- **bale out** 1 (*a*) (*leave by parachute*) The crew baled out (of the blazing plane). We shall have to bale out soon. (*b*) (*Sailing: expel incoming water*) They baled out desperately, to stop the boat sinking. 2 (*empty out*) You must bale out the water in the bottom of the boat or we will sink.
- **ball up** (*a*) (*make round*) He balled up the clay in his hand. (*b*) (*spoil, ruin*) It was his fault that the scheme failed, he balled up the whole thing.
- **band together** (*join together in a band or group*) They banded together to defend themselves.
- **bark out** (*shout out in a sharp or barking voice*) The sergeant barked out his orders.
- **barricade in** (*enclose with barriers*) They have barricaded the whole are in. The street was barricaded in. He has barricaded himself in with a shotgun and two hostages.
- **bash about/around** (*Fam: beat physically*) He bashes his wife about. The child has been badly bashed about.
- **bash in** (*a*) (*dent, severely*) The top of the box has been bashed in. (*b*) (*batter, beat in*) The gang bashed in his head.
- **bash up** (*smash badly*) He has bashed up his car. The gang bashed up his face. They said they would bash me up if I went to the police.
- **batter about/around** bash about.
- **batter down** (*knock down with heavy blows*) The men have battered down the door.
- **batter in** (*knock in by battering*) The men have battered in the door. The murderer battered in his victim's head.
- **battle on** (fight on, continue to do battle) (*a*) The army must battle on. (*b*) We must battle on against all opposition. (c) The ship battled on against the gale.

- **bawl out** 1 (*shout out loudly and raucously*) The steer bawled out in pain. 2 (*a*) (*shout out loudly and raucously*) The man bawled out his commands. He bawled out the news. (*b*) (*reprimand*) The colonel bawled us all out for inefficiency.
- **be + particle** (*be, with location*) Oh, if you're looking for her, she's about somewhere. If you want to see him, he's always in at six p.m. They are up in the attic, looking at some old pictures. He's down in the cellar, getting some coal. She's away in London at the moment. I'm afraid he's out, and won't be back till about midnight.
- **be above** (*be superior to*) He is above such petty things. She thinks she is above criticism. He is not above stealing to get what he wants.
- **be after** (*want, seek*) He is after promotion. I think she's after him, and not his friend. What are they after?
- **be along** (*appear, arrive*) He'll be along in a moment. Please have a seat, someone will be along soon.
- **be at** (*a*) She's at him all the time about his behaviour. (*b*) (*be occupied with, be doing*) He's at it again. They're hard at it, trying to get finished before nightfall. She's at this job day and night. (*c*) (*be happening*) This is where it's at, man.
- **be away** (*exclamation on departure of vehicle or aeroplane etc.*) It's away! They're away!
- **be back** (*return*) I'll be back in a few minutes.
- **be behind** 1 (*a*) (*be late or delayed*) I'm rather behind today (with my work/with the schedule). They are behind with their rent/payments. (*b*) (*be slow or retarded*) He's rather behind in his work at school. I'm afraid she's behind in her arithmetic. 2 (*be slow in relation to, be less capable than*) He's behind the others in his work.
- **be below** (*be below deck*) The captain is below.

- **be beneath** (*be too undignified /vulgar for*) He thinks it is beneath him to speak to ordinary workers.
- **be by** (*come near or past, pass by*) He'll be by in a moment and you can ask him yourself.
- **be down** (*a*) (*specifically, be down from a bedroom*) She'll be down in a moment. (*b*) (*be depressed, ill*) He's a bit down just now. She's down with flu.
- **be down for** (*have one's name down in a register for*) We are down for a new council house. He's down for promotion.
- **be down on** (*be critical of, be antagonistic towards*) I'm afraid they are rather down on him at the moment. She has always been down on them since they complained about her.
- **be in** (a) (*specifically, to be at home or in one's office, etc.*) She's in. He's in, but he's busy. (*b*) (*come in, arrive*) He'll be in shortly. The train will be in any minute now. (*c*) (*be elected or assigned to a post*) Their candidate is in. He's in now, and can get on with the job. (*d*) (*be in place or position*) The nails are in, so we can finish the work. The furniture's in, and the new house is beginning to look like home.
- **be in for** (*be due for, be in line for*) They are in for promotion. She is in for a surprise/shock. He'll be in for trouble if he goes on like this.
- **be in on** (*be party to, be fully involved in*) He is in on the whole sordid business. They were definitely in on the conspiracy. I'm sure she's in on their plans.
- **be in with** (*be in favour with, be friendly with*) He is in with her at the moment. She's (well) in with those people.
- **be on** (*a*) (*be fixed for a specific time*) The meeting is on. The party is on again, in spite of the problems. (*b*)

(*I accept your wager or challenge*) Okay, you're on! (*c*) (*be impossible, unacceptable*) Your suggestion is just not on, it's too expensive.
- **be on to** (*be on the track of, be aware of*) I think the police are on to his little game. The tax authorities will soon be on to your trick.
- **be out** (*a*) (*specifically, be out of the house or office etc.*) She's out, and I don't know when she'll be back. I'm afraid he's out. (*b*) (*be impossible*) What you suggest is quite out (of the question). It's out, I'm afraid. (*c*) (*be revealed, made public*) The news is out now. The scandal is out for all to see. (*d*) (*be published*) His book is out. (*e*) (*be blossoming*) The flowers are out. (*f*) (*be on strike*) All the workers are out.
- **be out for** (*be seeking*) He's just out for his personal gain. Those boys are out for trouble. He's out for everything he can get.
- **be over** (*a*) (*specifically, to be flying or moving over*) The bombers will be over soon, so we had better make for the shelters. (*b*) (*specifically, to come over or across*) He'll be over in a few minutes. The doctor will be over as soon as he can. (*c*) (*be finished, be at an end*) The play's over. Well, it's all over now. I can hardly believe it's all over. It's over and done with. (*d*) (*beyond the barrier, above the barrier etc*) The ball's over! The horse is over and still going strong.
- **be through** (*be finished*) She said they were through, and she'd give him back his ring.
- **be through with** (*be finished with*) She says she's through with men forever. I think he is through with that particular job.
- **be up** (*a*) (*specifically, to be out of bed*) He's up now. They are usually up by this time. (*b*) (*specifically, be up*

from a lower level) He's down in the cellar, but he'll be up in a few minutes. (*c*) (*of period of time: be finished*) Time's up, I'm afraid. Your half-hour is up, you must bring in the boat now. When three days were up he returned to town.

- **be up against** (*be faced with, be confronted with, be afflicted with*) He is up against very tough opposition in his work. She is up against it, now that her husband has died.
- **be up and about** (*a*) (*be active*) He's up and about every morning at dawn. (*b*) (*specifically, be active after an illness*) Yes, she's up and about again.
- **be up to** (*a*) (*be engaged, secretly, in*) I wonder what they are up to. I expect he's up to something (mischievous). Those boys are always up to something. (*b*) (*be able to, feel well enough to*) He has done, that work very, badly, I'm afraid he's just not up to it. She is getting better but still isn't up to going out yet.
- **be well up in** (*be expert in, be well-versed in*) She's well up in her subject.
- **bear + particle** (*bear or carry, with direction*) They bore in his body. The ambassadors to the emperor bore away great gifts. The envoy bore back to us tidings of war.
- **bear down (up)on** (*a*) (*steer dangerously towards*) The great ship bore down upon our helpless dinghy. (*b*) (*approach ominously*) The policeman bore down upon the small boys. The matron bore down upon the terrified nurses. (*c*) (weigh heavily on) This responsibility bears down on me. (*d*) (reprimand or punish) They will bear down heavily on you if you fail.
- **bear in** (up)on (*formal, bring to the attention of*) It was slowly borne in on me that he would never return. It must be borne in upon you all that such behaviour will not be tolerated.

- **bear off** (*a*) (*carry off, steal*) The raiders bore off many of the local girls. (*b*) (*win*) He bore off all the prizes.
- **bear out** (*support, confirm*) I hope you will bear out what I tell them. He will bear me out. I'm afraid that the results bear out my earlier suspicions.
- **bear up** (*carry on, continue to do the necessary things of life,, survive*) He bore up well under/against his father's death. How is she bearing up after her illness? Come on, bear up!
- **beat + particle** (*force by beating or striking, with direction*) We managed to beat the enemy back. They beat the birds out (of their cover). She tried to beat the mosquitoes away/off.
- **beat back** 1 (*go back, under sail*) The yacht beat back towards the shore. 2 (stop from advancing) The men tried to beat the flames back.
- **beat about** 1 (*turn about, under sail*) The galleon beat about, and headed for the Caribbean. 2 (*search*) They were beating about for him.
- **beat down** 1 (*fall hard, pour down*) The monsoon rains were beating down. 2 (*a*) (*reduce by haggling or outbidding*) They tried to beat the price down. That's my price and I'm sticking to it—you can't beat me down any further/anymore. (*b*) (*flatten*) The wind has beaten the corn down.
- **beat in** (*a*) (*batter or break in*) The police beat in the door. The gang beat his brains in.
- **beat out** 1 (*sail into the wind*) The sailing ship beat out to sea. 2 (*a*) (*sound by beating*) The drummers beat out a steady rhythm (*b*) (*extinguish by beating*) The men succeeded in beating out the fire.
- **beat up** 1 (*go up, under sail*) The dinghy beat up to windward. 2 (*a*) (*mix to a paste by beating*) She beat up

the eggs/cream. (*b*) (*beat savagely*) The gang beat him up and left him for dead. noun a beating-up. (*c*) (*summon*) The army is beating up recruits for the campaign. (*d*) (*seek strenuously*) The manager himself has gone out to beat up custom for the shop. She tried to beat up some support for the campaign she was leading. (*e*) (*exhausted*) I'm all beat up.

- **beckon + particle** (*beckon, or summon with direction*) She beckoned me in. The man stood there, beckoning us out. He beckoned her over, and showed her the books.

- **become of** (*happen to*) What will become of those refugees? What is to become of me if you go away? I don't know what will become of her.

- **bed down** 1 (*go to bed*) We bedded down for the night in a small inn near the mountains. I'm afraid we haven't a spare room but you can bed down on the settee. 2 (*a*) (*put to bed*) She bedded the children down without much trouble. He was bedded down with his brother. (*b*) (*settle for the night*) They bedded the horses down comfortably.

- **bed out** (*transfer o special flower beds in the open air*) The bulbs should now be bedded out.

- **beef up** (*reinforce, strengthen*) The army is to be beefed up by several divisions. The general has, decided to beef up the garrison.

- **beetle + particle** (*move like a beetle or with quick scuttling actions, with direction*) The little car beetles along quite well at 50 mph. The man beetled off to attend to the work. She beetled about, cleaning the house energetically.

- **belch out** 1 (*pour or billow out*) Smoke belched out from the volcano. Blue smoke belched out from the car's exhaust pipe. 2 (*emit*) The volcano belched out smoke and cinders. The car's exhaust belched out blue smoke.

- **belch up** (*emit by belching, regurgitate*) The volcano began belching up hot ash and cinders.
- **bellow out** 1(*a*) (*roar out*) The bull bellowed out in pain. (*b*) The sergeant bellowed his orders out.
- **belly out** (*swell out like a belly, billow out*) The sails bellied out in the strong breeze.
- **belt + particle** (*move rapidly, with direction*) The car was belting along at 90 mph. The motorbike belted past. The boys belted in, looking for something to eat.
- **belt out** (*a*) (*sing or pound out loudly*) The blues singer belted out the number. (*b*) They belted it out for all they were worth.
- **belt up** 1 (*a*) (*put belts on*) The soldiers belted up and went out. (*b*) (*be quiet*) I wish he would belt up. Oh, belt up, would you? Belt up! 2 (*fit up with or by means of a belt*) They belted the mechanism up.
- **bend + particle** 1 (*bend, lean with direction*) He bent down to pick it up. He bent over. The road bends away at that point. She bent back to escape being kissed. 2 He bent it back. She bent the corners over. Can you bend it in? He bent it backwards and forwards till it broke.
- **bend over** (*bend over to receive strokes, of a cane, on the buttocks*) The master told the boy to bend over.
- **billow out** (*a*) (*swell or belly out*) The sails billowed out as the breeze filled them. (*b*) (*pour out, usually in circling gusts*) The smoke billowed out of the wrecked tanker.
- **bind down** (*keep down by binding or tying*) They bound their prisoner down. He was bound down with cords. The surgical patient had to be bound down tightly before the operation, because movement was dangerous.
- **bind on** (*put on by binding*) She bound the pad on (to his arm) with a roll of bandage. He bound it on with tape.

- **bind over** (*enjoin, warn*) The magistrate bound him over to keep the peace. He has been bound over by the judge.
- **bind up** (*a*) (*seal or enclose tightly by binding*) She expertly bound up the wound. He bound the package up with tape. (*b*) (*completely enclose or wrap up*) My life is bound up in yours now. She is bound up in him, and won't listen to advice. (*c*) (*be absorbed*) He is completely bound up in the book he is writing. (*d*) (*connected*) One question is intimately bound up with another.
- **bite back** 1 (*bite in return*) The cat bit back. 2 (*a*) (*bite in return*) The little boy bit his friend, and got bitten back. (*b*) (*restrain*) She wanted to tell him her real feelings, but she bit the words back.
- **blab out** (*reveal carelessly in speech*) He blabbed out our secret. She always blabs out confidences.
- **black out** 1 (*become unconscious, faint*) I'm sorry; I just blacked out for a few minutes. 2 (*a*) (*make completely black or dark*) The city has been blacked out because enemy bombers are expected. *noun* a blackout (*b*) (*delete by making black*) He blacked out the words he didn't want.
- **blare out** 1 (*sound out brassily*) The trumpets blared out. The car horns blared out. 2 The car horns blared out their warnings. The trumpets blared out a fanfare. The radio loudspeakers blared the news out.
- **blast off** 1 (*take off with the power of jets or rockets*) The spaceship blasted off. The jet fighters blasted off from the deck of the aircraft carrier. 2 (*displace; remove or destroy by blasting*) The explosion blasted the roof off.
- **blaze away** (*a*) (*blaze or burn continuously*) The fire blazed away for a long time, without needing more fuel. (*b*) (*fire continuously*) The soldiers blazed away at the enemy positions.

- **blaze down** (*a*) (*send down great heat*) The sun blazed down pitilessly from a white sky. (*b*) (*come down blazing*) Cinders and ash blazed down from the erupting volcano. A bomber blazed down, out of control.
- **blaze out** (*a*) (*burn out violently or intensely*) A light blazed out from the window. Flames blazed out from the crater of the volcano. (*b*) Anger blazed out of her eyes.
- **blaze up** (*a*) (*burn up violently, or intensely*) The fire blazed up when he poured petrol on it. (*b*) Her anger blazed up when she was told what he wanted.
- **bleach out** (*a*) (*remove by using bleach*) She bleached the stains out (of the cloth). (*b*) (*fade*) The sunlight has bleached the colours out. The dress is old and has a bleached-outlook.
- **blink away** 1 (*blink, wink continuously*) That fellow just sits there, blinking away. 2 (*remove by blinking*) She said nothing, and tried to blink away her tears.
- **block in** (*a*) (*enclose with blocks*) The space has been blocked in. (*b*) (*trap, surround*) The car has been blocked in by all those lorries.
- **block out** (*a*) (*mark out in blocks*) The area has been blocked out, and building will begin soon. (*b*) (*stop from getting through*) That wall blocks out all the light.
- **block up** (*fill up, close up*) The traffic is very heavy, and has begun to block up the streets The drains are blocked up.
- **blossom out** (*a*) (*come out in blossom, develop fully*) The fruit trees have blossomed out beautifully. (b) She has blossomed out into a lovely young woman. His hopes seem to be blossoming out.
- **blot out** (*a*) (*erase by blotting*) He blotted out his mistakes. (*b*) (*Fig: kill, destroy*) The whole city has been blotted out by saturation bombing. He intends to blot

out all opposition. (*c*) (*erase*) He tried to blot out the memory of that embarrassing moment.
- **blow + particle** 1 (*blow, with direction*) the papers blew out. The leaves blew in. The smoke blew away. 2 The wind blew the papers out of the window. The breeze blew the leaves in. He blew away the cigar smoke.
- **blow down** (*a*) (*fell, knock down, demolish, by blowing*) The storm blew down many trees. The explosion blew several buildings down. (*b*) (*dislodge downward*) The wind has blown apples down. Soot has been blown down into the fireplace.
- **blow in** (*a*) (*implode, burst in*) The walls have blown in because of the pressure from outside. (*b*) (*arrive casually or unexpectedly*) Say, look who's just blown in!
- **blow off** (*remove or displace by an explosion*) They blew the door off with a small charge of gelignite: The shell had blown his head off.
- **blow out** 1 (*a*) (*billow out*) The curtains blew out as the wind caught them. (*b*) (*explode and stop functioning*) The electric fire seems to have blown out. *noun* a blow-out (*c*) (*explode outward*) The walls have blown out under the pressure from within. 2 (*a*) (*extinguish by blowing*) She blew out the candle. He blew the oil lamp out. (*b*) (*blast out*) The bombs should blow them out (of that bunker). 3 *noun* a blow-out=an expensive celebration. *Example:* They spent ₹ 1,000 on drink and had a real blow-out.
- **blow over** (*a*) (*pass, vanish*) It's a problem now, but I expect it will all blow over. It has blown over, and everything is back to normal.
- **board up** (*seal up with boards*) The shop is boarded up. They boarded the door up and went away.

- **bob + particle** (*move with bobbing actions, with direction*) the cork bobbed along in the water. Some debris was bobbing along on the tide. Some pieces of wood bobbed past. The children bobbed in and out among the trees.
- **bog down** 1 (*a*) (*get caught, as if in a marsh*) Your car will bog down in that mud. (*b*) The negotiations bogged down over the question of repatriating the prisoners of war. 2 (*a*) (*catch in a bog or in mud*) This rain will bog all the cars down in the field. (*b*) The question of the prisoners will bog the negotiations down.
- **boil away** 1 (*a*) (*boil continuously*) The water was boiling away in the kettle. (*b*) (*boil until none left*) All the water boiled away and the kettle was ruined. 2 (*remove or eliminate by boiling*) They boiled the excess liquid away.
- **boil down** (*render down or decompose by boiling*) They boil down horses' hoofs to get glue.
- **boil down to** (*can be reduced to*) It all boils down to whether you want to go or not. The whole question boils down to the old debate about free will and determinism.
- **boil over** (*a*) (*spill over after boiling*) The milk in the pan boiled over onto the cooker. (*b*) Tempers have begun to boil over and there will be trouble.
- **boil up** 1 (*a*) (*come up boiling*) Lava boiled up from the crater of the volcano. (*b*) Trouble is boiling up in the ghettos. 2 (*bring to boiling point*) The stew must be boiled up before serving.
- **bolster up** (*support, prop up*) The government needs bolstering up. He expects us to bolster up his reputation. She takes gin to bolster up her courage/to bolster her up.
- **bolt + particle** (*move suddenly and quickly, with direction*) The hare bolted off, with the hounds on its tail.

He bolted away to find them. The cat bolted out when it saw the dog.
- **bolt back** (*hold or fix back with bolts*) They bolted the shutters back.
- **bolt on** (*fix on with bolts*) They bolted the handles on.
- **bolt down** (*a*) (*fix down with bolts*) He bolted the hatch down. (*b*) (*swallow quickly*) He just bolts his food down.
- **bolt up** (*close completely by means of bolts*) They bolted up the doors.
- **bomb out** (*a*) (*bomb thoroughly*) The city has been bombed out. It is an old bombed-out building. (*b*) (*force to leave by bombing*) We shall bomb them out of that place. They were bombed out of three houses during the war.
- **bone up on** (*learn, swot up*) I'll have to bone up on my German.
- **book down** (*put down in a book, register*) He booked us down for the next ship.
- **book in** 1 (*give name or information for a register*) Where do we book in? Those people haven't booked in yet. 2 (*a*) (*receive or accept by putting name or information in a book*) They haven't been booked in. I don't think the receptionist has noticed them. (*b*) (*reserve or obtain a place for*) Let's book him in at the Grand Hotel.
- **book out** 1 (*state departure by entering name in a book*) I'll book out for both of us. 2 (*confirm departure by entering name in a book*) He booked me out. We didn't know that she books people out.
- **boom out** 1 (*sound out with a booming noise*) The ship's foghorn boomed out. 2 (*say in loud booming tone*) He boomed out his greetings.
- **boost up** (*a*) (*raise by pushing upwards*) He boosted his friend up to look over the wall. *Example:* Give

me a boost-up please, I can't reach it. (*b*) (*reinforce, strengthen*) The prestige of the government has been boosted up by this victory. The engine has been boosted up considerably. I hope you will be able to boost up the morale of the soldiers.

- **boot + particle** (*a*) (*move by kicking with a boot, with direction*) He booted the ball over. They were booting an old can about. The centre-forward booted the ball in. (*b*) The troublemakers were booted out.
- **border (up)on** (*a*) (*tie on the border of*) The new housing estate borders upon the playing-fields. (*b*) (*verge on, touch on, come near to*) His action borders upon insubordination. The soldiers' behaviour borders on mutiny. This kind of risk borders upon insanity.
- **boss about/around** (*order about*) I don't like being bossed about by you or anyone else. Stop bossing me about! He thinks he can come in and boss everybody about.
- **botch up** (*spoil completely*) He has botched up our plans. I wish you wouldn't come along and botch everything up. Don't botch it up this time.
- **bottle up** (*a*) (*seal in a bottle*) She bottled up all the gooseberries for the winter. (*b*) (*seal as if in a bottle*) She bottles up her emotions. The tension in the family is caused by everyone bottling up their feelings. Don't bottle it up. Speak out.
- **bounce + particle** 1 (*bounce, rebound, with direction*) The ball bounced back. It bounced up and down. She bounced in with the good news. He bounced out excitedly. 2 She bounced the ball along. He bounced it up and down.

- **bounce out** (*a*) (*eject by force*) They bounced the troublemakers out of the hall. (*b*) He has been bounced out of every bar in town.
- **bound + particle** (*bound or leap, with direction*) He bounded past. The kangaroos bounded along. The boys bounded about.
- **bow down** (*a*) (*intensive of bow*) The envoy bowed down low. (*b*) (*submit*) We shall not bow down to this disgrace.
- **bowl + particle** (*roll steadily, with direction*) The car bowled along smoothly. They bowled up in a new car. They bowled back to town in his Rolls-Royce.
- **bowl out** (make to leave the game through the ball striking the wicket) The batsman was bowled out.
- **bowl over** 1 (*a*) (*knock over with a bowl*) He bowled the skittles over. (*b*) (*knock over*) The car bowled the gatepost over. He came running round, the corner too quickly and bowled the old lady over. (*c*) (*astonish*) I was completely bowled over by his proposal.
- **box in** (*enclose with a box or something like a box*) They boxed the garden in with fences. I feel boxed in here because of the design of the houses.
- **box off** (*mark off or separate in a box or box-like plan*) They have boxed the area off into separate sections.
- **box up** (*put in boxes, package*) The goods have been boxed up and are ready to go.
- **brace up** 1 (*prepare or steady oneself*) He braced up for the bad news. Come on, old chap, brace up! 2 (*make steady or more secure*) They braced up the old building with baulks of timber. A whisky will brace you up a bit. Brace yourself up!

- **branch off** (*diverge, take a separate route*) The road to the coast branches off from the main road in about a mile. We'll have to branch off shortly to get to the village.
- **branch out** (*diversify, develop a new line*) They are branching out into textiles. She began as an artist but she has branched out and is making toys now as well.
- **brave out** (*endure*) She has braved out the gossip and rumours. You'll just have to brave it out for a time.
- **brazen out** (*resist and dismiss insolently*) She brazened out the scandal. Trust him to brazen it out, as if nothing had happened.
- **break away** 1 (*a*) (*come away in pieces*) The surface is rotten and breaks away when you touch it. (*b*) (*rebel*) I imagine he will try to break away. The state has broken away from the union. 2 (*remove by breaking*) They broke away the veneer with a chisel.
- **break in** 1 (*enter illegally*) A burglar broke in during the night. 2 (*a*) (*knock in smash in*) The men broke the door in with axes. He broke in the top of the box. (*b*) (*tame*) It will be difficult to break that horse in. (*c*) (*help adjust*) I shall give you an easy job just to break you in to the work.
- **break into** (*a*) (*enter illegally, enter by stealth*) The burglar broke into the house. (*b*) (*burst into, begin to exude*) He broke into a cold sweat. (*c*) (*suddenly*) They broke into song. (*d*) (*interrupt*) He broke into our argument/discussion.
- **break off** 1 (*a*) (*break or sever an engagement to marry*) They've broken off. (*b*) (*stop for a rest or break*) Let's break off for ten minutes. (*c*) (*interrupt oneself*) He broke off and didn't start again. 2 (*a*) (*knock off*

by breaking) He broke the handle off. She broke the top off by accident. (*b*) (*sever, discontinue*) They have broken off the negotiations/talk. She has broken off the engagement.
- **break (off) with** (*have no further relations with*) I intend to break with these people. She broke off with him long ago.
- **break out** 1 (*a*) (*escape from a place*) The prisoners have broken out. (*b*) (*appear, start suddenly*) War broke out in 1914. Cholera has broken out in Bengal. 2 (*a*) (*get out by breaking*) He broke the panels out. (*b*) (*take out of store*) I'll break out some of that 1954 vintage, to celebrate.
- **break out in** (*exhibit suddenly*) The child has broken out in spots. He has broken out in a rash. *Example*: There was an outbreak of measles in the school.
- **break through** 1 (*a*) (*force a way through*) The soldiers have managed to break through (*b*) (*achieve something new, make a major advance*) The biologists claim to have broken through in a new area of genetics. 2 (*force a way through*) The soldiers broke through the enemy lines.
- **break up** 1 (*a*) (*disintegrate*) The formation has broken up. Their partnership has broken up. *noun* breakup= disintegration. (*b*) (*disband*) School has broken up for the holidays. 2 (*a*) (*reduce by breaking*) He broke up the soil. The prisoners were breaking up rocks. (*b*) (*stop*) He broke up the fight between the two gangs. Come on, break it up! (*c*) (*destroy, upset completely*) This trouble has really broken him up.
- **breathe away** (*breathe continuously and freely*) He breathed away deeply for a few minutes, to recover from the effort.
- **breathe forth** (*breathe out, emit*) The dragon breathed forth fire.

- **breathe in** 1 (*inhale*) Breathe in deeply and hold your breath please. 2 (*take in by breathing*) The workers inevitably breathe in poisonous fumes.
- **breathe out** 1 (*exhale*) He breathed out. 2 (*a*) (*emit by breathing*) He breathed out whisky fumes. (*b*) (*whisper*) He breathed out their names just before he died.
- **breeae + particle** (*go like a breeze, with direction*) He breezed in to see her. They breezed off somewhere. He breezes about in a little sports car.
- **brick in** (*enclose with bricks*) The area has been bricked in.
- **brick over** (*cover over with bricks*) The surface has been bricked over.
- **brick up** (*seal up with bricks*) They bricked up the windows to keep children out of the derelict house. It looks like an old bricked-up doorway.
- **bridge over** (*link with a bridge*) The gorge has been bridged over. They will bridge it over with planks.
- **brighten up** 1 (*a*) (*become bright or brighter*) The sky brightened up after the storm. (*b*) (*become more lively*) The party brightened up when the pop group arrived. 2 (*a*) (*make bright or brighter*) She brightened up the room with some colourful curtains. (*b*) (*make more lively, liven up*) They brightened the party up with some music and dancing.
- **bring + particle** (*bring, with direction*) He brought the box in. She brought her mother out to the car. They will bring some friends over. I want to bring her along to see you.
- **bring about** (*a*) (*Naut: turn completely*) He brought the ship about and headed for safety. (*b*) (*cause to happen*) This accident has been brought about by your recklessness.

- **bring down** (*a*) (*cause to be reduced*) Their demands have brought the prices down. After much hard bargaining he brought the trader down to Rs 100 for the carpet. (*b*) (*cause to be defeated, defeat*) Their action may yet bring the government down. This scandal could well bring him down.
- **bring forth** (*a*) (*produce*) He brought forth a new plan, just as unworkable as the old one. (*b*) (*give birth to*) She brought forth twins.
- **bring forward** (*a*) (*advance, propose*) She brought forward a new proposal. (*b*) (*advance in time*) They have brought the meeting forward to next Monday. (*c*) (*Bookkeeping: bring into next column etc.*) Have you remembered to bring forward the profit from last month?
- **bring in** (*introduce*) He intends to bring in some reforms. The government is bringing in new legislation on this matter. You with have to bring in some outside help or you will never get the job finished in time.
- **bring off** (*a*) (*rescue, take of successfully*) The coastguards have brought all the crew off, and the ship is sinking by the bows. (*c*) (*complete successfully*) He brought the deal off in a spectacular way. Trust her to bring it off.
- **bring on** (*a*) (*introduce, on a stage*) He brought on the guest speaker, amid applause. (*c*) (*cause*) This kind of weather often brings on hay fever. The trouble might bring on her headaches again. I hope your experience doesn't bring on anything nasty.
- **bring out** (*a*) (*develop*) Her teacher wants to bring out her talent. (*b*) (*evoke*) This kind of work brings out the best in him. (*c*) (*coax to be less shy*) She may be able, to bring him out a bit, but it won't be easy. (*d*) (*publish*) The

company intends to bring out a new series of educational books. (*e*) (*introduce into the market*) They are bringing out a new brand of soap powder next month.
- **bring through** (*a*) (*conduct safely through*) He brought his party through without accidents.
- **bring together** (*a*) (*bring into contact*) He likes bringing young people together. (*b*) (*unite*) Fate has brought them together. Emergencies often serve to bring people together. (*c*) (*re-unite*) I'll do what I can to bring them together, but it won't be easy.
- **bristle out** (*stick out or protrude with or like bristles*) His beard bristled out aggressively. The porcupine's quills bristled out.
- **bristle up** (*a*) (*stick up with or like bristles*) His hair bristled up The hair on the dog's neck bristled up. (*b*) (*become angry*) She bristled up when I suggested that the job wasn't suitable for her. He bristles up very easily.
- **brown off** (*bore, frustrate*) This kind of job really browns me off. I'm browned off with working so hard for so little money.
- **brush + particle** (*move with a brush, sweep, with direction*) She brushed the dirt out. He brushed the hairs off. They brushed the leaves away.
- **brush aside** (*discard, wave aside, treat as unimportant*) He brushed aside all our objections. I don't like being brushed aside like this.
- **brush away** (treat as neither important nor desirable) He brushed the whole business away. You can't just brush it away like this!
- **brush off** (*reject*) He brushed off all our suggestions. I didn't expect her to brush us off like this. *noun* a brush-off.

- **brush over** 1 (*a*) (*brush fully*) He brushed the coat over. 2 (*treat lightly, almost ignore*) He brushed over the details of policy.
- **brush up** (*a*) (*brush thoroughly, clean thoroughly with a brush*) You should brush the place up a bit. (*b*) (*improve*) I want to brush up my Italian. He wants to brush up his knowledge of electronics.
- **brush up against** (*a*) (*touch lightly*) I brushed up against her unintentionally. (*b*) (*encounter*) He has brushed up against trouble.
- **brush up on** (*revise, improve*) I must brush up on my French before I go to France.
- **bubble + particle** (*move, in, with or like bubbles, with direction*) Water began to bubble up. The stream bubbled away down the hill. We watched the hot liquid bubbling out. The boiling milk rose up and bubbled over.
- **buck off** (*throw off by bucking*) The horse bucked its rider off.
- **buck up** 1 (*a*) (*be or become more cheerful*) This news will make him buck up a bit. Oh, buck up, things could be worse. (*b*) (*hurry up*) Buck up or we'll be late! 2 (*make more cheerful*) This news should buck you up. Your help has bucked me up a lot.
- **buckle down** 1 (*get to work*) You'll just have to buckle down and show that you can do it if you want. He expects you to buckle down to the job whether you like it or not. 2 (*fix down with a buckle or buckles*) He buckled the harness down. The equipment was firmly buckled down.
- **buckle on** (*fix or put on with buckles*) The soldiers buckled their equipment on. He buckled the horse's harness on.

- **buckle to** (*get busy*) They buckled to and got the work done.
- **buckle up** (*put on with the buckles tight or secure*) The soldiers buckled up their equipment. Everything is buckled up.
- **build in** (*fix in, in a permanent way*) The cupboards are built in to the walls of the house. It will not be difficult to build wardrobes in if you want them. *noun* built-in cupboards. *Idiomatic:* He's been so long with that firm you'd think he was built in with the bricks.
- **build on** (*add on as a new part*) We can build an extension on later if you want one. The annexe has been built on to the main building.
- **bulge out** (*intensive of bulge*) Her swollen abdomen bulged out. The contents of the bag began to bulge out.
- **bum along/about/around** (*go about like a tramp or bum*) He just bums along, living from day to day.
- **bumble + particle** (*go in a particularly clumsy, incompetent way, with direction*) He bumbles about, doing everything wrong. They bumble in without warning from time to time. He will bumble through somehow.
- **bump + particle** (*move with a bumping noise, with direction*) The body bumped along as they pulled it. You could hear something bumping about upstairs. The car bumped down on to the road from the pavement.
- **bump off** (*kill, murder*) A gang of thugs bumped him off. Be careful they don't try to bump you off next.
- **buy over** (*win over by paying money*) The enemy may try to buy you over. He seems to think he can buy us over very cheaply.
- **buy up** (*obtain by buying as widely as possible*) They have been buying up all available land. Speculators are trying to buy up supplies of raw materials.

- **buzz away** (*a*) (*fly away with a buzzing noise*) The bee buzzed away. (*b*) (*buzz continuously*) The bees were buzzing away among the clover. The machine buzzed away for more than an hour.
- **buzz off** (*go away*) I told them to buzz off. Buzz off, can't you see I'm busy!

C

- **call + particle** 1 (*call, with direction*) He called out when he saw her. She called across to me. He called down from the top of the ladder. 2 (*summon by calling, with direction*) I called him over to tell him the story. She called me aside to tell me the bad news. He was called away by his friends.
- **call back** 1 (*re-contact*) Thanks for the news, I'll call back in half an hour. 2 (*a*) (*summon*) He was called back from his holiday to handle the problem. (*b*) (*re-contact*) I'll call you back when I get more information.
- **call down** 1 (*a*) (*summon from below*) They called her down from upstairs to answer the telephone. (*b*) (*summon, as from God*) The old man called down curses on the heads of those who disbelieved. (*c*) (*reprimand*) They really called me down for doing that.
- **call for** (*a*) (*summon, demand*) The customers called for more beer. (*b*) (*collect*) I'll call for you at seven o'clock and we can go there together. She called for the books she had lent me. (*c*) (*demand, require*) This job calls for a man of considerable initiative. The work calls for endurance and patience. The present situation calls for entirely new measures.

- **call forth** (*demand, bring into play*) The emergency called forth reserves of energy which she did not know she possessed.
- **call in** 1 (*a*) (*summon to a place*) They decided to call in a doctor, because the child was no better (*b*) (*require to be brought in*) The library is calling in all outstanding books. The bank has begun to call its money in.
- **call off** (*a*) (*abandon, cancel*) The workers have decided to call off their strike action. The businessmen suddenly called the deal off. He phoned me and called the appointment off. (*b*) (*prevent from attacking*) The dog frightened me until its master called it off.
- **call out** 1 (*a*) (*summon from a place*) They called out the guard to investigate the noises. Someone called out the fire brigade on a false alarm. We hope it will not be necessary to call out the army. Doctors are often called out in the middle of the night. (*b*) (*summon to a duel*) He has called out his rival, and they are meeting at dawn tomorrow. (*c*) (*summon to strike*) The trade union officials have called their members out (on strike).
- **call over** 1 (*visit casually*) He called over to see us yesterday. 2 (*a*) (*call in sequence*) They called over all the names on the list.
- **call round** (*visit casually*) He says he'll call round at about eight.
- **call up** 1 (*a*) (*summon' bring in*) The general called up reinforcements. (*b*) (*mobilise*) The army is calling up reservists in case of emergency. *noun* call-up=legal summons to join the armed forces *noun* call-up papers. *Example:* He got his call-up papers yesterday =he received notice that he must report for military service. (*c*) (*contact*) I'll call you up if I need your help.

- **call (up)on** (*a*) (*visit*) They called on me yesterday for about an hour. (*b*) (*visit for a special purpose*) The deputation called upon the mayor to invite his co-operation in their work. (*c*) (invite, exhort) We called upon him to speak at the meeting. (*d*) (*invoke*) The men called upon God to help them. The government hopes that it will not be necessary to call upon emergency powers.
- **calm down** 1 (*become calm, quiet*) I expect she'll calm down in a few minutes, when she gets over the shock. 2 (*make calm*) I tried to calm him down after the bad news.
- **camp out** 1 (*live in a camp or tent*) The boys like camping out in good weather. The battalion camped out on the plain. 2 (*to house in tents or a camp*) The men were camped out near the town.
- **cancel out** (*a*) (*delete*) Next, you should cancel out all the noughts. (*b*) (*annul, eliminate, neutralise*) I'm afraid your present behaviour cancels out any past help you gave us. The two things are so opposed that they just cancel each other out.
- **caper + particle** (*leap and jump in a light-hearted manner, with direction*) The children were capering about in the garden. The clowns capered up to us laughing and joking.
- **care for** (*a*) (*look after, attend*) She has been caring for her invalid mother for many years. (*b*) (*like*) I don't really care for that sort of thing. I don't much care for sweets. Would you care for a cup of tea? She doesn't care for him anymore.
- **career + particle** (*move very rapidly, often dangerously, with direction*) The car was careering along at a terrific speed. The huge machine came careering down on us.
- **carry + particle** (*carry, with direction*) She carried the box up to the attic. He carried the tray in. The butler carried the empty bottles away.

- **carry away** (*transport, enchant*) He was carried away with childish enthusiasm. Take your time and think carefully—don't get carried away! I'm afraid he got carried away and forgot what he was doing.
- **carry back** (*a*) (*transport to an earlier time*) Ah, that music carries me back. The sight of the place carried her back to her childhood.
- **cast aside** (*a*) (*throw away, discard*) I refuse to be cast aside in this manner. You can't just cast people aside like old clothes.
- **cast away** (*a*) (*jettison*) The men cast away the equipment they would not need. (*b*) (*abandon, maroon*) The people had been cast away on a desert island for ten years n a castaway= a marooned person.
- **cast back** 1 (*look back*) He cast back in his mind to the last war, trying to remember exact dates. 2 (*direct to the past*) He cast back his mind to earlier days. She cast her thoughts back to happier times.
- **cast down** (*a*) (*lower, throw down quickly*) She cast her eyes down shyly. *adj* downcast (*lowered*) She sat with downcast eyes. (*b*) (*demoralise, discourage*) I feel rather cast down at the moment. *adj* downcast= (*sad*) Don't look so downcast, it might not be so bad. He was very downcast when he got the exam results.
- **catch on** (*a*) (*catch, grab*) The child kept catching on to his mother's skirt. (*b*) (*become popular*) this is a nice tune and I think it'll catch on quickly. (*c*) (*understand*) He is no fool he'll catch on soon enough to what you are doing.
- **catch out** (*a*) (*discover, trap*) Be careful, or they'll catch you out telling lies. He was caught out cheating in the exam. (*b*) (*be eliminated from the game through the ball being caught in the air*) the batsman was caught out after only one run.

- **catch up** 1 (*succeed in pursuing*) (*a*) (*Lit*) You'd better drive faster, because the others are catching up quickly. (*b*) I expect he'll catch up on lost time by working harder. She says she just can't catch up with her work. 2 (*a*) (*lift and keep in position*) She caught up her hair into a bun. (*b*) (*pick up quickly*) He caught up the ball as it rolled along and threw it back.
- **cave in** (*a*) (*collapse*) The roof of the old mine is dangerous and could cave in at any time *noun* a cave-in=a collapse. (*b*) (*yield abjectly*) the opposition expect the government to cave in on this issue, but I don't think they will. He caved in under the weight of her complaints. Enemy resistance soon caved in.
- **cavort + particle** (*move in a playful, skipping manner, with direction*) The young horses cavorted along. I saw the kids cavorting about in the garden.
- **chain up** (*restrain by means of a chain*) The guard dogs are kept chained up until evening, when they are released.
- **chalk out** (*a*) (*mark out or delineate with chalk*) He chalked out a design on the blackboard. The girl chalked out a game on the ground. (*b*) (*outline clearly*) the general began to chalk out a plan of campaign.
- **chance (up)on** (*meet by accident*) I chanced upon him last week for the first time in years.
- **change down** (*go down one gear while driving*) The driver changed down from third to second (gear). The driver changed down quickly.
- **change into** (*a*) (*transform oneself into*) The witch changed into a frog. (*b*) (*put on*) Just let me change into something less formal. You must change into a clean dress before we go out.
- **change over** (*make a conversion*) We have just changed over from gas to electricity. The mechanism changes

over automatically *noun* a change-over. *Example:* The change over to decimal currency went very smoothly.
- **change up** (*go up one gear while driving*) The driver changed up from third to top (gear). The driver changed up too soon and the car stalled.
- **channel off** (*divert by means of or through a channel*) (*a*) (*Lit*) The engineers channeled the water off without difficulty. (*b*) (*divert*) they tried to channel off some of the revenue earmarked for armaments and use it to alleviate poverty.
- **charge + particle** (*attack at a run or a gallop; move suddenly and forcefully, with direction*) The cavalrymen charged down on the defenceless villagers. The boy charged up and asked for an ice cream. The bull charged out into the sunlight of the arena.
- **charge up** (*a*) (*credit*) Please charge the meal up to the company. I'll charge the expenses up. (*b*) (*provide an electrical charge for*) the man in the garage said he would charge up my car battery.
- **charm + particle** (*impel to move or do, by using charm, with direction*) He could charm the birds out of the trees. She managed to charm the little boy down from the top of the ladder.
- **charm up** (*a*) (*use charm on*) If you charm him up a bit, I'm sure he'll do what you want.
- **chart out** (*a*) (*mark out on a chart or map*) The navigators charted this area out and it's quite safe to sail in it. (*b*) (*explore*) they hope to chart out that particular area of the Amazon.
- **chase + particle** (*pursue, with direction*) She chased the cat out into the garden. The boy chased his sister in and out among the bushes.
- **chase down** (*a*) (*follow one drink with another*) He chased the whisky down with a pint of beer.

- **chop up** (*cut up with sharp strokes*) (*a*) He chopped up some wood for the fire. (*b*) (*divide*) they have apparently decided to chop the company up into smaller units.
- **chuck + particle** (*throw casually, with direction*) He chucked away the empty tin. They clicked out a lot of old furniture. She chucked the materials up to him.
- **chuck out** (*a*) (*eject forcibly, expel*) They chucked him out of the college for being a bad influence.
- **chuck up** (*a*) (*abandon, resign from*) He has decided to chuck the whole thing u. He chucked up the work and went to another town.
- **chug + particle** (*move, accompanied by the noire of an engine, with direction*) The ship chugged along. As we neared the harbour, a small boat came chugging out. A steam train chugged past.
- **chum up** (*become friends, pal up*) Those two seem to have chummed up pretty quickly. She chummed up with another new girl.
- **churn away** (*continue to churn, shake*) The wheels of the paddle- steamer churned away, causing the water to swirl up.
- **churn up** (*against by churning*) The wheels of the trucks have churned up a lot of mud.
- **circle round** (*move around in circles*) The hawk slowly circled round in the sky, watching its prey. Wolves circled around, waiting.
- **clam up** (*close one's mouth tight, like a clam; become silent*) They are afraid he's going to clam up on them. Don't clam up just when the story is getting interesting.
- **clamber + particle** (*climb heavily or clumsily, with direction*) The boy clambered slowly up onto the roof. The men clambered carefully along the mountainside. I hope you don't expect me to clamber down there.

- **clamp down** (*close, down tightly into position*) He clamped the metal lid firmly down.
- **clamp down on** (*suppress, restrain*) The government may find it necessary to clamp down on such activities. *noun* a clampdown = a severe restriction. *Example*: During the emergency there was a clamp-down on news from abroad.
- **clap on** (*a*) (*encourage to come on, by clapping*) The audience clapped her on. (*b*) (*put on firmly*) He clapped his hat on angrily and walked out. (*c*) (*add*) The men clapped on more sail, to take advantage of the fresh wind. (*d*) (*apply*) the driver clapped on his brakes when he saw the child.
- **clap out** (*exhausted or finished*) He was driving a clapped-out old car. I feel really clapped out today.
- **clap to** 1 (*close noisily*) The door clapped to. 2 (*close noisily*) He clapped the door to.
- **clean down** (*clean thoroughly, in downward direction*) He cleaned the lorry down last night.
- **clean out** (*a*) (*clean thoroughly*) He cleaned out his room. (*b*) (*strip, empty*) The robbers cleaned the bank out, and got away with Rs. 100,000. (*c*) (*leave with no money*) We played cards and he cleaned me out.
- **clean up** 1 (*a*) (*clean the place*) She had to clean up after the children's party. *noun* a clean-up (*b*) (*be successful, make a great profit*) He certainly cleaned up on that deal. *noun* a clean-up. 2 (*a*) (*clean thoroughly*) She cleaned the place up after the children's party. (*b*) (*reform*) The new mayor said he would clean the city up a clean-up.
- **cleanse away** (*completely clean or purify*) They cleansed away all the filth. The preacher promised that God would cleanse away all their sins.
- **clear away** 1 (*a*) (*vanish*) The mist cleared away as the sun came out. (*b*) (*clear the table*) Mother always clears

away quickly when we have finished eating. 2 (*remove*) The engineers began by clearing away the debris. Mother cleared the dirty dishes away when we had finished eating. Clear away your toys now, children!

- **clear off** 1 (*go away*) I told them to clear off. Clear off! 2 (*a*) (*settle*) He has at last cleared off all his debts. (*b*) (*redeem*) I hope to clear off my mortgage in a few months' time. (*c*) (*dispose of*) The manager wants to clear off all the old stock in the warehouse.
- **clear out** 1 (*a*) (*clean by clearing thoroughly*) He cleared out the cupboards. *noun* a clear-out. (*b*) (*remove, evict*) He cleared the people out of the room. They have cleared all the tenants out of those houses.
- **climb + particle** (*move by hands and feet, with direction*) I watched the men below climbing up. He said he would climb down and help them. I opened the window and he climbed through.
- **climb down** (*a*) (*compromise*) I expect they'll climb down if you show them you are determined. (*b*) (*admit defeat*) They had to climb down when they saw the evidence.
- **clock in/on** (indicate time of one's arrival at work by putting a card in a machine with a clock) The men clock in at this time every day.
- **clock off/out** (indicate time of departure from work by putting a card in a machine which stamps the time on the card.) The men clock off at this time every day.
- **clock up** (*a*) (*indicate time, speed etc. by using a clock*) He clocked up 150 km/h on the straight in that car. He has now clocked up more overtime than any other man in the factory. (*b*) (*gain, achieve*) I expect he'll clock up quite a few successes in the next year or two.
- **clog up** 1 (*become closed through clogging or filling with soft material*) The water pipe has clogged up again.

2 (*close through clogging*) The mud has clogged up the pipe. The sewers are all clogged up.
- **close down** 1 (*close without intention of re-opening*) That little shop on the corner has closed down. The radio station closed down for the night. *noun* a closedown. 2 He has closed down his business in London. They have decided to close that branch down.
- **comb out** (*a*) (*comb completely*) She combed out her long hair. (*b*) (*remove by a combing action*) She combed the lice out of the child's hair.
- **come + particle** (*come, with direction*) He opened the door and came out. She opened the door and came in. He told the children to come along. He said he would come back in half an hour.
- **come about** (*a*) (*change direction*) The wind has come about in the last hour. The ship came about and headed back for safety. (*b*) (*happen*) How does it come about that you are here, and not in London?
- **come across** 1 (*a*) (*cross*) He came across to where we were standing. (*b*) (*be received, make an impression*) His speech came across well/badly. 2 (*find or meet by chance*) If you come across my book, will you send me it? I came across him by chance one day last week.
- **come across with** (*provide*) He came across with Rs. 10 just when I needed it. The informer came across with the names of his accomplices in the bank robbery.
- **come apart** (*disintegrate*) The machine came apart when he started it up. I'm afraid the thing just came apart in my bands.
- **come at** (*a*) (*find, get hold of*) I've been looking for that article, but can't come at it anywhere. (*b*) (*determine, discover*) It's difficult to come at the exact facts. (*c*) (*attack, approach in a threatening way*) The man came at me with a knife.

- **come away** (*a*) (*leave*) She had to come away before the end of the play. Come away from that window! (*b*) (*become detached*) My heel has come away from the rest of the shoe. The woodwork has come away.
- **come back** (*a*) (*return*) He came back two hours later. Now, to come back to what I was saying a moment ago. (*b*) (*return to one's memory*) His face is coming back to me now. (*c*) (*of fashion, to be popular again*) Short skirts are coming back. (*d*) (*reply vehemently*) When charged with the crime, he came back at us furiously. When accused of theft, he came back with a stinging counter—accusation.
- **come down with** (*a*) (*become ill from*) He has come down with influenza. (*b*) (*pay out*) She has come down with Rs 15 at last.
- **come down (up) on** (*a*) (*punish, rebuke*) The government intends to come down heavily on tax evaders. He came down on me like a tonne of bricks. (*b*) (*pounce on*) They came down on me for a subscription to their association.
- **come forward** (*present oneself*) He has come forward with an offer of help. She has come forward as a candidate in the local elections.
- **come from** (*originate from*) He comes from Turkey. This word comes from Latin.
- **come in** (*a*) (*enter*) She opened the door and came in (*b*) (*arrive*) When does your train come in? (*c*) (*become seasonable*) When do strawberries come in? (*d*) (*tome to be fashionable*) I expect long skirts will come in again soon. (*e*) (*flow in*) The tide comes in a long way at this point. (*f*) (*join the game*) The batsmen came in. (*g*) (*take position in a race or competition*) He came in fourth. (*h*) (*be elected to power*) The socialists came in at the

last election. (*i*) (*be received as income*) He has ₹ 5,000 coming in every year. (*j*) (*have one's place or work*) Where do I come in, in your scheme?

- **come in for** (*receive, suffer*) I'm afraid they come in for a lot of abuse from some people. She came in for a lot of criticism.
- **come into** (*inherit*) He has come into a lot of money from his old uncle's estate.
- **come near to/come close to** (*get close to*) I came near to telling him just what I thought of the whole business. I came close to screaming because of the din. He came close to committing suicide.
- **come of** (*a*) (*result from*) Nothing came of it, I'm afraid. That's what comes of disobeying the instructions. (*b*) (*be descended from*) He comes of a good family. These racehorses come of excellent stock.
- **come out in** (*exhibit, of symptoms*) He came out in a rash last night. She has begun to come out in spots. I came out in a cold sweat.
- **come out of** (*emerge from, survive*) He has come out of the ordeal well.
- **come out with** (*say*) He comes out with some funny ideas. When I asked her where she had been, she came out with some story about visiting her aunt. You never know what that child will come out with next.
- **come over** (*a*) (*cross over to visit*) You really must come over sometime and have dinner with us. (*b*) (*come from a distance, usually across a sea*) He came over from France last week, just to see us. They come over from New York every spring. (*c*) (*become, suddenly feel*) I came over all dizzy just for a moment, but I'm all right now. She came over queer.

- **come round** (*a*) (*visit casualty*) He came round (to see us) last night. (*c*) (*regain consciousness*) The unconscious man slowly began to come round. (*d*) (*begin to accept or appreciate something*) I think he'll come round eventually.
- **come round to** (*begin to accept or appreciate*) She is slowly coming round to our point of view.
- **come through** (*a*) (*survive*) I hope he will come through all right, despite the danger. Not many men in that regiment came through.
- **come together** (*converge*) The two lines come together at that point.
- **come up to** (*a*) (*reach the height of*) He's getting big, and comes up to my shoulder now. (*b*) (*attain, fulfill*) Do you think he will come up to expectations in that new job of his? This work hardly comes up to the required standard.
- **come up with** (*produce*) He came up with a good idea for getting the lawnmower working again. She has come up with some fine suggestions.
- **conceive of** (*a*) (*imagine*) I can't conceive of anything funnier than that. (*b*) (*consider*) He wouldn't conceive of her going to London at her age. I refuse to conceive of such a solution to our problem.
- **conduct + particle** (*convey or escort, with direction*) He asked the guard to conduct us out. The receptionist conducted us in to meet the great man.
- **conjure away** (*remove by conjuring or magic, make disappear*) (*a*) The magician conjured the rabbit away. (*b*) I don't trust him, and feel as though he's going to conjure all the money away. She thinks that the doctor can just conjure headaches away.

- **conjure up** (*make appear by conjuring or magic*) (*a*) The magician conjured up a white rabbit. (*b*) The situation was desperate, but the general could hardly conjure up fresh reinforcements from nowhere. (*c*) (*cause to appear*) Some people claim to be able to conjure up the spirits of the dead. (*d*) (*evoke*) This scent conjures up many pleasant memories.
- **coak out** (*stop functioning*) I'm afraid the engine has conked out.
- **contract in** (*enter by contract or arrangement*) I'd like to contract in on this project, if I may.
- **contract out** (*leave by contract or agreement*) I'd like to contract out of this project, if you don't mind.
- **cook-out** (*a barbecue or similar outdoor cooking*) We had a cook-out in the garden yesterday.
- **cook up** (*a*) (*prepare by cooking quickly*) She cooked up an omelette and chips when he arrived unexpectedly. (*b*) (*invent, fabricate, concoct*) To avoid going to the meeting he cooked up an excuse about being ill. I don't like cooking up stories just to help you out of a difficult situation.
- **cough up** 1 (*provide money or information*) I don't think he'll cough up unless you put pressure on him. 2 (*a*) (*emit while coughing*) He began to cough up blood. (*b*) (*provide*) He wouldn't cough up the cash when we asked for it.
- **count down** (*count backwards to zero, to reach a required time*) The controllers counted down to blast-off. **noun a countdown.**
- **count for** (*signify*) That doesn't count for much in this country. He seems to count for quite a lot in his firm.
- **count in** (*a*) (*include by counting*) He has counted all the guests in. (*b*) (*include*) Please count me in on this project. You can count me in. We have counted you all in.

- **count on** 1 (*continue to count*) He counted on monotonously until he reached 100.
- **count up** 1 (*intensive of count*) Count up to ten before you open your eyes. 2 (*a*) (*enumerate*) They began to count up their losses after the battle. (*b*) (*total*) The men counted the money up carefully.
- **count (up)on** (*depend on, rely on*) We are counting on you to help. I had counted upon having it completed by March.
- **couple up** (*join by linking*) The railway men coupled up the wagons.
- **crack down** (*come down or descend with a cracking noise*) The whip cracked down on the horse's rump.
- **crack down on** (*suppress*) The general cracked down on any sign of mutiny. You should crack down on these people before real trouble starts. *n* a crackdown.
- **crack up** 1 (*break into pieces*) (*a*) The soil is cracking up because of the drought. (*b*) I must be cracking up, because I'm beginning to forget everything I should be doing. 2 (*consider, claim*) This material isn't all it is cracked up to be.
- **crawl + particle** (*crawl, with direction*) The baby crawled along. A spider was crawling up into the pipe. They crawled down to rescue the injured miners.
- **cream off** (*a*) (*remove the cream from*) She creamed off the milk. (*b*) (*remove as the best*) This educational system creams off the most promising pupils (from all the others).
- **crop up** (*a*) (*Geol*)=crop out. (*b*) (*emerge, arise*) Some difficult questions crop up at this point. The same problems keep cropping up all the time. Something has cropped up and I won't be home tonight till late.

- **cross off** (*eliminate from a list*) Ha crossed their names off as they answered him.
- **cross out** (*delete from a sheet of paper*) He crossed the word out and wrote in another. Don't cross it out until you are sure you don't want it.
- **cycle + particle** (*move on a bicycle, with direction*) The women cycled along. The workmen cycled off home. The boy cycled away, whistling.

D

- **dab on** (*apply in small quantities*) She dabbed on the ointment with cotton wool. The child dabbed on the paint with her finger.
- **dam up** (*a*) (*seal with a dam*) They have dammed that river up. (*b*) (*contain, restrain*) He dammed up his fury until he could no longer remain silent.
- **damp down** (*reduce in strength by making damp*) She damped the fire down for the night.
- **dance + particle** (*dance, with direction*) 1 She felt she could dance on forever. The people were dancing about in the village square. The girl danced up to us and gave us some flowers. They danced out in a kind of procession. 2 He danced her out on to the verandah.
- **dart + particle** (*move suddenly and quickly; with direction*) The snake darted forward. The thief darted back into the shadows. Some figures darted past. Men were darting in and out among the trees.
- **dash + particle** (*run quickly or recklessly, with direction*) He dashed in breathlessly. She dashed out without telling us where she was going. He has dashed off somewhere. The boy dashed away to meet his friends.

- **dash down** (*throw down violently*) He dashed the cup down in his anger.
- **dash off** (*write or produce quickly or casually*) He just dashed the poem off. She dashed off two articles before dinner. I'll just dash off a letter to him.
- **date back** (*go back in time to a particular date*) This manuscript dates back to the 8th century.
- **daub on** (*dab on heavily, smear on*) The witchdoctor daubed on thick blotches of paint. She certainly daubs her make-up on. Some artists like to daub their colours on with a palette knife.
- **daub over** (*cover over heavily*) He daubed the canvas over with paint.
- **dawdle away** (*waste*) He has been dawdling his time away. We dawdled away three hours playing poker.
- **dawn (up) on** (*come as a realization to*) It has slowly dawned upon us that he will not help. It dawned on him that he was no longer as young as he used to be.
- **deck out** (*decorate, dress*) They are decked out in their sunday best. He is decked out for some kind of party. She's all decked out and ready to go. The ship was decked out with flags and bunting.
- **deliver up** (*surrender*) The captain has delivered up himself and his men to the enemy. They have delivered up the city.
- **dice away** (*lose by dicing or gambling*) He diced his fortune away at the casino.
- **die away** (*diminish or dwindle*) The sound of the car died away in the distance. The echoes died away.
- **die down** (*a*) (*decrease, lose force*) The wind has died down a bit. The fire has died down. Towards evening the noise dies down. (*b*) (*Fig: decrease, diminish*) The

protests of the students are beginning to die down. His anger has died down a bit.
- **die off** (*become extinct*) The species is dying off. It would be a pity if these birds are allowed just to die off.
- **die out** = **die off**. (*cease to be*) The fire died out.
- **dig away** 1 (*dig continuously*) He has been digging away for hours. 2 (*detach, loosen or displace by digging*) Animals have dug away the whole bank at this point. The workmen have dug away the foundations.
- **dig in** 1 (*a*) (*dig trenches and similar defences*) The soldiers have dug in along the river. (*b*) (*start eating*) Okay, dig in! The boys dug in ravenously. 2 (*a*) (*introduce into the earth by digging*) The gardener dug the compost in.
- **dig into** (*a*) (*eat heartily*) They dug into the meal. (*b*) (*investigate thoroughly*) The detectives are digging into this whole business.
- **dim out** (*cause to fads out, make dim*) The lights of the city have been dimmed out because of the power cuts. *noun* **a dim out** = a time when lights are dimmed out.
- **din in** (*force or push in*) We have been trying to din some sense in to him. Given time with him, his teachers may din something in.
- **dine in** (*eat dinner at home*) They are not going out, but intend to dine in tonight. The students always dine in at their college on Thursdays.
- **dine out** (*eat dinner in a restaurant*) We sometimes dine out at one of our favourite places.
- **dip in** (*immerse briefly or lightly*) He dipped his finger in, to test the heat of the water.
- **dip in to** (*read small parts of, for pleasure*) I dip into this book whenever I can.

- **direct + participle** (*order, recommend or. guide, with direction*) The policeman directed us across to the information office. He was directed up to the waiting-room by a receptionist.
- **dish out** (*a*) (*semi out in a dish or dishes*) She dished out the food. (*b*) (*supply*) They enjoy dishing out advice to everyone. He can dish out as much criticism as he gets.
- **dish up** (*a*) (*serve up in a dish*) She dished up the stew. (*b*) (*serve up, with or without dishes*) She can dish up a lovely meal when she wants to. (*c*) (*provide*) He dished up a lot of useful facts and figures.
- **dispense with** (*do without*) We can dispense with his help.
- **dispose of** (*remove, get rid of*) They disposed of the rubbish.
- **dither about/around** (*move about, trying ineffectually to do something*) She dithers about half the time, getting in everyone's way. Oh, stop dithering about!
- **dole out** (*hand out as a dole or charity*) The food was doled out to the refugees. They dole out just enough for each family. The government doles out something to help the victims of emergencies. You can't expect us to dole out money like a public charity.
- **doll up** (*dress up smartly*) She dolled herself up for the party. They are all dolled up and ready to go.
- **double + particle** (*move at double pace, with direction*) The soldiers doubled along, carrying all their equipment. He doubled over to where the victims lay.
- **double back** 1 (*return on exactly the same route*) The hunters doubled back the way they had come. 2 (*fold back*) She doubled back the bedclothes.
- **doze off** (*fall asleep*) The old man dozed off by the fire. Oh, I must have just dozed off for a minute or two.

- **draft out** (*write out a preliminary version*) He drafted out his letter of resignation. Can you draft out a plan for us?
- **drag + particle** (*pull, with direction*) He dragged the bags along behind him. The children have dragged all their toys out again. The cat has dragged something in. We dragged them apart to stop the fight.
- **drag down** (*a*) drag. (*b*) (*debilitate*) His illness is dragging him down.
- **drag in** (*introduce with an effort*) Why must you always drag this subject in when we are talking?
- **drag on** (*last an unpleasantly long time*) The meeting dragged on.
- **drag up** (*a*) (*introduce unpleasantly*) Must you drag up all these old scandals? (*b*) (*raise badly*) These children appear to have been dragged up rather than brought up.
- **drain off** 1 (*run off through some kind of drain*) The liquid has drained off into the ground. 2 (*remove through some kind of drain*) They have drained off the liquid they want.
- **draw + particle** (*pull, with direction*) He drew the cloth away. She drew the curtains back. He drew the blinds down. The croupier drew the money in. The barman drew off a pint of beer.
- **draw apart** 1 (*separate*) Husband and wife have drawn apart over the months. These wooden covers draw apart if you pull them. 2 (*a*) (*pull apart*) You can draw the covers apart if you wish. (*b*) (*take to one side*) He drew me apart to tell me what he had heard.
- **draw away** (*a*) (*move off*) The car drew away as we approached. (*b*) (*move ahead*) The faster car drew away. The best runner was beginning to draw away. (*c*) (*isolate oneself*) She has drawn away lately and we can't find out why.

- **draw back** (*a*) (*move backwards*) The cat drew back as we approached. (*b*) (*withdraw, retire*) She has drawn back from us all and we don't know why.
- **draw down** (*a*) (*bring down*) She has drawn down blame on her own head. They seek to draw down ridicule on us.
- **drift + particle** (*move aimlessly, with direction*) The rudderless boat was drifting along on the current. The wreckage slowly drifted away. Something was drifting up on the tide. Those boys drift about doing nothing. He has drifted back and forth between Europe and Asia several times.
- **drill down** (*dig or bore down with a drill*) The prospectors have been drilling down into the bedrock, hoping to strike oil.
- **drink away** 1 (*drink continuously*) He has been drinking away for hours. 2 (*relieve by taking alcoholic drink*) He is trying to drink his trouble away. You can't drink your sorrows away. He tried to drink the memory away.
- **drink down** (*drink in one gulp*) He drank the draught down. His mother got him to drink the medicine down. Come on, drink it down!
- **drink in** (*a*) (*absorb readily*) These plants just drink the water in. The dry soil drinks the rain in. (*b*) (*absorb, receive with rapture*) The children just drink in his stories. She stood and drank in the panorama.
- **drink off** (*quaff, drink in one long swallow*) He drank off the flagon of wine amid their cheers.
- **drink up** 1 (*drink until finished*) She told the children to drink up. The barman asked the men to drink up. Drink up! 2 (*drink until all gone*) Children, drink up your milk.

- **droop down** (*flag, hang down*) The flowers drooped down to the ground, because of the heat.
- **drop across** (*come across to visit*) Drop across and have coffee sometime.
- **drop away** (*a*) (*fall sheer*) The cliff drops away at that point. (*b*) (*become less*) The attendance has dropped away in recent months.
- **drum up** (*summon*) They are trying to drum up public enthusiasm for the candidate. He can't drum up any support for his plans.
- **dzy down** (*dry completely*) He dried himself down after a shower.
- **duck down** (*intensive of duck*) The soldier ducked down behind a wall as bullets began to fly.
- **dust down** (*a*) (*dust completely, clear completely of dust*) She dusted down the furniture. After his fall he rose and dusted himself down. (*b*) (*Fame reprimand*) The colonel dusted his men down for inefficiency. *noun* a **dusting-down**= a severe reprimand.
- **dust off** (*clean off by dusting, sweep the dust from*) She dusted off the hat and put it on.
- **dust out** (*clean out by dusting*) She dusted out the cupboards.
- **dust-up** (*a quarrel*) *Example*: There was a bit of a dust-up at the office, about who was to do what.
- **dwell (up)on** (*spend time on, discuss too much*) I have no wish to dwell upon the unpleasant side of this business. He dwelt upon all the nasty aspects with considerable satisfaction.
- **dwindle away** (*diminish, become smaller or fewer*) The money has just dwindled away to nothing. The numbers attending these meetings have dwindled away terribly.

E

- **ease + particle** (*ease, move slowly and gently, with direction*) He eased the screws out of the old wood with great care. The nurse eased away the bandage from the wound.
- **ease off** (*remove slowly and gently*) The nurse eased the bandage off. He eased the stamp off carefully.
- **eat away** 1 (*eat steadily or continuously*) They have been eating away for more than an hour. 2 (*destroy by, or as if by, eating*) The acid has been rating away the sides of the container. The sea water is eating away the base of the cliff. The rats have eaten the woodwork away. This part has been eaten away by insects.
- **eat in** (*eat at home*) We aren't going out, we're eating in tonight. Most of the students eat in.
- **eat into** (*destroy, through action of acids etc.*) The substance has begun eating into the woodwork.
- **eat out** (*dine in a restaurant*) We need a baby-sitter tonight, because we are eating out. It's a long time since she last ate out.
- **eat up** 1 (*eat until all finished*) Come on, children, eat up! 2 (*a*) Come on, children, cat up your food! (*b*) (*devour, consume*) This car just cats up the miles. The central heating eats up a lot of electricity.
- **ebb away** (*a*) (*flow away from a given position*) The tide ebbed away, leaving behind seaweed and debris. (*b*) Her enthusiasm slowly, ebbed away. He felt his strength ebbing away.
- **echo + particle** (*resound, with direction*) The shot echoed out. Her shout echoed back from the mountain.

- **edge + particle** (*move hesitantly or in small stages, with direction*) The cat edged along, its eyes fixed on the bird. The suspicious-looking fellow edged up to us, and asked us for money. The climbers edged slowly down from the summit of the mountain.
- **edge out** (*supplant*) They have been trying to edge him out of his position of power for several years. In the last election they succeeded in edging their opponents out (of office) by a small margin.
- **edit out** (*remove by editing*) He edited out the offensive paragraph.
- **egg on** (*encourage*) They egged him on to fight those other boys. We don't want to do it, so stop egging us on.
- **eke out** (*extend or maintain by care, rationing, etc.*) We must try to eke out our water supply until help comes. She ekes Out a living somehow. Please try to eke the money out till the end of the month.
- **elbow + particle** *Idiom*: to elbow one's way=to push with the elbows in order to pass. The men elbowed their way back into the crowd. He elbowed his way over to where we stood.
- **empty out** 1 (*empty completely*) The tank slowly emptied out. 2 He emptied out the tank. They emptied their pockets out, to show that they had no weapons.
- **end off** (*finish*) We ended the work off with a flourish.
- **end up** (*a*) (*come to an end, unsatisfactory*) If you drive your car like that, you'll end up in hospital. They ended up after five years with nothing to show for their effort. (*b*) (*finish by*) I ended up (by) telling him everything although I tried not to. Despite his strenuous efforts, he ended up unsuccessful after all.

F

- **face about** (*turn completely round*) He told the men to face about. Face about!
- **face out** (*resist, oppose*) You should face out your problems. He's a bully, but you'd better face him out straight away. He managed to face out their objections.
- **face up to** (*confront, accept*) He faced up to the problem. These are dangers which you must face up to. She doesn't like facing up to things. He won't face up to the fact that he is too old for the job.
- **fade in** 1 (*come in slowly until clear*) The scene faded in. Fade in to a scene in the office. 2 (*bring in slowly until clear*) Fade the scene in now. *noun* **a fade-in**.
- **fade out** 1 (*fade completely, die out*) (*a*) The picture on the TV screen suddenly faded out. The sounds faded out gradually. (*b*) (*Cine, TV*) Fade out to the next scene. (*c*) (*vanish, become obsolete or defunct*) These practices have faded out. 2 (*Cine, TV*) Fade the scene out and then fade in to the street scene. *n* a fade-out.
- **fag away** (*work hard and continuously*) He fags away for a pittance.
- **fag out** (*tire, exhaust completely*) This work will fag you out. Don't fag yourself out on their account. I'm really fagged out.
- **faint away** (*faint completely*) When she saw him she fainted (clean) away.
- **fake up** (*invent, fabricate*) He faked up the whole thing none of it was true. The painting was beautifully faked up.
- **fall about** (*laugh hysterically*) They were falling about (laughing).

- **fall away** (*a*) (*fall out and down*) The stones have fallen away from the side of the house. (*b*) (*sink or go down*) The ground falls away steeply at this point. (*c*) (*dwindle, diminish*) The number of people coming to the club has fallen away a lot. Attendances are falling away steadily. The old customs have fallen away into discuse.
- **fall back** (*a*) (*recoil*) He fell back in surprise. She fell back in dismay when she saw him. (*b*) (*retreat*) The army has begun falling back to prepared lines of defence.
- **fall back (up)on** (*go back to for support, have as a reserve*) We have some money to fall back on. It's good to have a friend to fall back upon.
- **fail behind** (*a*) (*fail to maintain one's position*) The racehorse fell behind. Several of the runners fell behind in the race. (*b*) (*fail to maintain a schedule*) She is falling behind with her payments for the cooker. They fell behind with the rent.
- **fall down** (*a*) (*fall to the ground or downward, drop*) The injured horse fell down. He fell down dead. (*b*) (*be in a state of dereliction*) That building is falling down. The house is falling down from lack of attention. (*c*) (*fail, come to nothing*) His plans have fallen down. (*d*) *Idiom*: He has fallen down on the job=he has failed.
- **fall for** (*a*) (*accept as true, be duped by*) Don't tell me you fell for that old trick! Everyone seems to fall for his charming manner. (*b*) (*become keen on*) She has fallen for him (in a big way). I have quite fallen for this year's purple colours.
- **fall in** (*a*) (*fall into something*) The child was near the river and I was frightened he would fall in. Be careful you don't fall in. (*b*) (*collapse inwards*) The walls fell in. They are afraid that the whole building will fall in

on them. *noun* **a fail-in.** (*c*) (*make or join the ranks or a parade*) He ordered the men to fall in. Fall in! (*d*) (*expire*) The lease of the land has fallen in. His debts have fallen in.
- **fail in with** (*accept, agree with, concur with*) I have decided to fall in with your plan. They have fallen in with the general policy. (*b*) (*join, associate oneself with*) He has fallen in with some strange people.
- **falter out** (*say or speak hesitantly*) She faltered out her name. He faltered out something about being lost.
- **fan out** (*a*) (*spread out like a fan*) The searchers fanned out across the mountainside, to cover as much ground as possible. He ordered the men to fan out. Fan Out! (*b*) The cards were fanned out face downward on the table. He fanned his search party out across the hills.
- **farm out** (*a*) (*pass on responsibility*) She farmed the children out on her neighbours. (*b*) (*delegate, distribute*) The work has been farmed out to various people. We must stop them farming out the inebriation to all the other agencies. (*c*) (*exhausted for farming*) This land has been farmed out. The area was farmed out long ago.
- **fasten down** (*fix down*) The windows have been fastened down. He fastened down the collar of his coat. They fastened the flaps down.
- **fasten on** (*fix on*) She fastened the badge on. Fasten it on here, please. Is it firmly fastened on to the saddle?
- **fasten up** (*do up, fix into place by fastening*) She fastened the dress up. Fasten up the buttons, please. Can you fasten me up, please?
- **fasten (up)on** (*latch on to, adopt quickly*) She fastened upon his suggestion as an excuse for her actions. Don't fasten upon his ideas so uncritically. She fastened upon the idea of going to London.

- **fathom out** (*understand, explain, comprehend*) I just can't fathom out his intentions. She couldn't fathom him out at all.
- **fatten up** (*make fat, for sale*) They are fattening the sheep up. These animals need fattening up.
- **fatten out** 1 (*become fat*) He has fattened out a lot. Those sheep have fattened out since I last saw them. 2 (*increase in quantity, lengthen*) It isn't a large piece of work, and needs fattening out.
- **fawn (up)on** (*flatter slavishly, ingratiate oneself with*) They like to fawn upon great writers. She fawns upon anyone with influence.
- **feast away** 1 (*feast continuously*) They were feasting away in the great hall. 2 (*spend in feasting*) They intended to feast the night away.
- **feed back** (*return in stages*) He fed the information back to us. The machine feeds back everything you need to know. *noun* **feedback**= (*i*) the return of specific information. (*ii*) the information obtained from operating anything, used to improve, correct or control further operations.
- **feed in** (*introduce steadily*) He fed the tape in (to the machine). Feed the wire in here. If you feed the data in, you get the analysis a few minutes later.
- **feed up** (*feed as fully as possible*) She fed him up on the best food she could get. We'll have to feed you up after your illness.
- **feel about/around** (*search about by touching*) He felt about in the dark for the door handle. She felt about for the light switch.
- **feel for** (*sympathise with*) I really feel for him in all these troubles. He felt for her in her sorrow.

- **feel up to** (*feel capable of, feel equal to*) He doesn't feel up to the job. I don't feel up to things today. We could go on now if you feel up to it.
- **fence in** (*a*) (*enclose with a fence*) He fenced hi his land. The area has been fenced in. (*b*) I feel fenced in by all these restrictions. Don't fence me in.
- **fence off** (*a*) (*separate with a fence*) He fenced off the whole plot of land. The area has been fenced off. (*b*) (*parry or resist*) He fenced off their attack/the blow. The speaker neatly fenced off the question.
- **fend off** (*parry, resist, deflect*) (*a*) He was able to fend off the blow with his arm. Nothing could fend off that attack. (*b*) The speaker fended off the questions.
- **ferret about/around** (*search about*) The police ferreted about for clues. He has been ferreting about, trying to get some information.
- **ferret out** (*elicit, bring out like a ferret*) He managed to ferret out quite a lot of information. She'll ferret it out for us if it's humanly possible.
- **figure out** (*a*) (*work out, estimate*) I can't figure out how much money I owe them. (*b*) (*work out, understand*) She figured out how he had arranged the matter. I wish I could figure out how their minds work. She couldn't figure him out at all.
- **file + particle** (*walk in line, with direction*) The men filed away silently. I watched the soldiers file out. Silent mourners filed past, paying their last respects.
- **file away** 1 (*scrape continuously with a file or abrasive tool*) He field away at the metal bar. 2 (*put away in a file or filing system*) The secretary filed the letter away.
- **file down** (*reduce by filing, or by means of a file*) He filed the surface down. The end of the bar had been field down to a point.

- **fill out** (*a*) (*fill with wind etc*) The sails filled out as the breeze caught them. (*b*) (*get fatter*) He has filled out a lot since I last saw him. Her cheeks have filled out.
- **fill up** 1 (*fill with petrol*) He filled up at the next petrol station. 2 (*a*) (*fill to the full*) She filled his glass up a second time. (*b*) (*fill the tank with petrol*) Fill her up! *noun* **a fill-up.**
- **film over** (*become covered with a thin layer*) The windscreen has filmed over with some kind of oil.
- **filter + particle** 1 (*a*) (*pass through a filter or in small quantities, with direction*) Water has begun filtering through into the bottle. The liquid filters out into this receptacle. (*b*) The soldiers filtered up one by one into the enemy position on the hill. News has filtered down to us that there is trouble among the directors. 2 We think the stuff can be filtered off without difficulty. The impurities have been filtered out.
- **find out** 1 (*discover the truth*) She is afraid he will find out. I hope she doesn't find out. 2 (*a*) (*discover*) They have found out the truth. If you do try to see her, be careful you're not found out. She will find out all his secrets. I finally found out what he was really like. (*b*) (*make enquiries about*) Will you try to find out when the trains leave? Find out his address, please.
- **fine down** (*smooth or file down until very fine*) The craftsman fined the wood down very gently.
- **finish up** (*finish completely*) Oh, finish it up now! I wish he would finish the whole thing up and forget about it.
- **fire away** 1(*a*) (*fire or shoot continuously*) The troops were firing away at the advancing enemy. (*b*) (*begin, sat telling a story*) We're ready to listen, so fire away!
- **firm up** 1 (*become solid*) The ground has firmed up a lot since it was properly drained. 2 (*make secure*) We should

try to firm this arrangement up a bit before putting money into the scheme.
- **fish for** (*seek*) She is always fishing for compliments. There's no good fishing for information, I can't tell you anything.
- **fish out** (*a*) (*bring out like a fish*) He fell into the river and we had to fish him out. They fished a lot of rubbish out (of that pool). (*b*) (*bring out*) He fished out a piece of string from his pocket. (*c*) (*be exhausted of fish*) The lake was fished out long ago. This river is in danger of being fished out.
- **fit on** 1 (*adhere, go into position*) This bottle top won't fit on. The catch of the door doesn't fit on any more. 2 (*put or fix on*) The dressmaker fitted the dress on and made some minor adjustments. The carpenter fitted some extra books on.
- **fit out** (*equip*) The ship has been fitted out with a new engine. The warship was fitted out with bigger guns. We must fit the expedition out with the best equipment.
- **fit up** (*a*) (*fix or put up*) The carpenter fitted up the wall cupboards. (*b*) (*fit, fix completely*) The place has been fitted up with all modern conveniences (all mod cons). It's well fitted up.
- **fix on** 1 (*choose, select*) They finally fixed on 2 p.m. as the best time. Well, we'd better fix on a date for the meeting. 2 (*fit or put on*) Can you fix this lid on, it keeps coming off. Fix the top on firmly. He fixed the badge on at the correct angle.
- **fix up** 1 (*arrange*) We've fixed up to go out tonight. They have fixed up to visit us next month. I fixed up to go abroad for a holiday. I have fixed up for a plumber to come tomorrow. 2 (*a*) (*fit or put up*) The carpenter fixed up the wall cupboards. (*b*) (*arrange*) I'll try to fix

something up that suits everyone. Let's fix it all up now. (*c*) (*provide an opportunity or work for*) Can you fix him up? They fixed me up with this job. (*d*) (*accommodate*) They fixed him up in a small hotel. Can you fix her up for the night?

- **fizz up** (rise while fizzing or effervescing) The lemonade fizzed up.
- **fizzle out** (*come to nothing, usu abjectly*) (*a*) The firework didn't work properly, but just fizzled out. (*b*) His schemes seem to have fizzled out. I hope the whole project doesn't just fizzle out. All his enthusiasm soon fizzled out.
- **flag down** (*stop, by using a flag, or making a flagging action*) The guards flagged the car down. He flagged the taxi down.
- **flake off** (*come off in flakes*) The paint has begun to flake off. The surface is flaking off.
- **flake out** (*a*) (*faint*) She flaked out when she heard the news. (*b*) (*fall instantly asleep through exhaustion*) They just flaked out when they got back.
- **flame out** (*burst out in flames, flare out*) A beacon flamed out against the night sky.
- **flame up** (*a*) (*burst out in flames, flare up*) The fire flamed up instantly. (*b*) His anger flamed up again.
- **flap + particle** (*fly with flapping wings, with direction*) The big bird slowly flapped away. Birds were flapping about everywhere. The vulture flapped off.
- **flare up** (*a*) (*burst into fire, come up in a sudden glow*) Lights flared up in the darkness. The bonfire flared up as I poured petrol on to it. (b) His temper flared up when he heard how much money had been spent. Trouble may flare up at any time in the city. *noun* **a flare-up** = a burst of fire/anger/trouble.

- **flash + particle** (*move very fast, or with a flash, with direction*) The car flashed past. He flashed in to tell us what happened, then flashed out again. They flashed off somewhere in their new car.
- **flash about/around** (*exhibit, display*) They are always flashing their money about. I wish she wouldn't flash her diamonds about so much.
- **flash back** (*a*) (*return or revert briefly to an earlier point in the story*) The film suddenly flashed back to the hero's youth. *noun* **a flashback** = a device for taking a story back in time. *Example*: There was a flashback to his youth.
- **flash-forward** (*a*) (*move briefly to a later point in a story*) The film flashed forward to show the deaths of the soldiers. *noun* **a flash-forward** = a device for taking a story on in time. *Example:* The author likes an occasional flash-forward to show the results of a character's decisions.
- **flatten out** 1 (*become flat or flatter*) The countryside flattens out beyond that ridge. 2 (*make flat or flatter*) She flattened out the dough with a rolling pin. The road roller flattened out the bumps in the road.
- **fling out** (*discard, disposes of*) He flung out everything he didn't need.
- **flip + particle** (*toss, jerk, with, direction*) He flipped the cigarette across to me. She flipped the cigarette ash off onto the floor. He flipped the stone over with his foot.
- **flip through** (*examine rapidly*) She flipped through the book. He flipped through the papers but could not find what he was looking for.
- **flit + particle** (*move lightly, with direction*) Butterflies were flitting in and out among the bushes. I watched a brilliant little bird flit past. The little girl was flitting

about in the garden, picking flowers. The figure flitted off into the darkness.
- **float + particle** 1 (*move on, or as on, a liquid, with direction*) The raft floated away. Something was floating in on the tide. I watched the rudderless dinghy float past. 2 They floated the boat off when the tide came in. We managed to float the barrels out to the ship.
- **flock + particle** (*move in a crowd*) People were flocking in from the surrounding countryside. We all flocked out to watch the display. Crowds were flocking past. Pilgrims flocked up towards the hilltop shrine. The children flocked round to listen. The sheep flocked together for warmth.
- **flood + particle** (*a*) (*move like a flood, with direction*) The water flooded back. The waves came flooding in. (*b*) The sunlight flooded in when she opened the curtains. People were flooding in from the surrounding countryside. Men and women flooded out into the streets.
- **flood out** 1 (*inundate*) The rains may flood the place out. The villages were flooded out. 2 (*force to leave a place through flooding*) We were flooded out (of the house).
- **flop + particle** (*move with clumsy actions, with direction*) The dying fish flopped about on the riverbank. The tired girl flopped down in a comfortable chair. The head of the doll flopped back and forth grotesquely.
- **flow + particle** (*a*) (*flow, with direction*) The water flowed past. The tide flowed in rapidly. He watched the liquid flow out. (*b*) Resources are flowing out too fast. Profits began to flow in later the same year *n* overflow, inflow, outflow.
- **flounder + particle** (*flounce, move in a manner, with direction*) She flounced out in a huff. The girls flounced in to show their new dresses.

- **flounder + particle** (*a*) (*flounder, move sluggishly, ineffectually, with direction*) Stop floundering about and think of something to do I We floundered along in the mud. (*b*) He floundered on in his bad French. I suppose she'll flounder out of her problems somehow.
- **flush away** (*dispose by means of a rash of water*) He flushed the waste materials away.
- **flush out** (*a*) (*clear or clean out by flushing*) She flushed the sink out with warm water. Flush the bottle out (thoroughly) before re-using. (*b*) (*remove or expel by flushing*) He flushed the dirt and stones out with a hosepipe. All the rubbish has been flushed out. (*c*) (*expose, bring out of concealment*) The police intend to flush the bandits out. The security forces say they will flush out all the troublemakers.
- **fly apart** (*come apart violently, disintegrate under pressure*) The machine shook so much that I thought it would fly apart. The engine flew apart while they were testing it.
- **fly into** (*suddenly develop or exhibit*) He flew into a rage. Now, don't fly into a temper with me!
- **fly off** (*come off suddenly and/or violently*) The wheel flew off and narrowly missed me. I'm afraid in case bits start flying off when the engine starts!
- **fly past** (*a*) (*fly past information*) The aeroplanes flew past. *noun* **a fly-past**=a ceremonial flight, part of a military display or parade.
- **foam up** (*come or pour up foaming*) The froth and bubbles foamed up. When he poured the warm beer, it foamed up (out of the glass).
- **fob off** (*a*) (*cheat, placate temporarily*) He intends to fob us off again. Stop fobbing everyone off with false

promises. (*b*) (*palm off, pass with deliberate deception*) Are you trying to fob this rubbish off on us? You aren't fobbing inferior goods off here!

- **fold back** 1 (*fold to one side or out of the way*) The bed folds back. 2 (*put back by folding*) She folded back the bedclothes. Fold back the shutters, please.
- **fold down** 1 (*go flat by folding*) The flap folds down. 2 (*put down by folding*) Fold the flap down. He folded down the corner of the page.
- **fold up** 1 (*a*) (*end in failure*) The business folded up. The play folded up. Most of his ambitious schemes fold up on him. (*b*) (*double up*) He folded up with laughter. 2 (*make smaller by folding*) She folded up the papers. Fold up your clothes tidily please.
- **follow on** 1 (*a*) (*continue to follow*) He followed on despite every difficulty. (*b*) (*continue*) The story follows on from the death of the heroine. The later books follow on from the earlier ones. We shall follow on from where he left off. 2 (*come on after*) He goes on (to the stage) first, and then you follow him on.
- **forge ahead** (*a*) (*make good progress*) The ship forged ahead under a favourable wind. (*b*) The students have forged ahead with their work. She seems to be forging ahead in her new job.
- **fork out** 1 (*pay, unwillingly*) I had to fork out again, to get her what she wanted. He doesn't like forking out. 2 (*a*) (*remove or expel with a fork*) He forked the weeds out. (*b*) (*pay, provide, unwillingly*) I don't like forking out any more money than absolutely necessary. He won't fork out a penny more.
- **fork up** 1 (*pay up, unwillingly*) Come on, fork up! 2 (*a*) (*dig up and loosen with a fork*) He forked up the soil.

- **foul up** (*a*) (*make dirty*) The whole river has been fouled up with oil. This place has been really fouled up. Trust that dog to foul the place up! (*b*) (*spoil*) They have really fouled up their chances of success. The whole business has been fouled up by his stupidity. Trust him to foul things up!
- **frame up** (*a*) (*put in a frame*) We must frame up that picture (*b*) *noun* **a frame-up**= a faked impression that someone has committed a crime, whereas in fact he has not. *Example*: I didn't do it, it's a frame-up!
- **fray away** (*fray slowly*) The rope has been frayed away and could snap if pulled suddenly.
- **freak out** (*have a drug trip, have hallucinations*) He freaked out for several hours. *noun* **a freakout** = a state of drug-induced hallucination.
- **freeze in** (*restrict to a place through freezing weather conditions*) The whole village was frozen in for a week. The ship was frozen in as the ice thickened.
- **freeze off** (*show no enthusiasm for*) He offered his help, but they froze him off. They froze off his offers of help.
- **freeze on to** (*attach oneself to*) He froze on to them aid wouldn't go away.
- **freeze over** (*become covered with ice*) The lake froze over. Even the river froze over that winter.
- **freeze up** 1 (*freeze completely*) The whole village froze up. The water pipes froze up. 2 (*freeze completely*) We were frozen up last year and had burst water pipes afterwards. *noun* **a freeze-up**.
- **fret away** (*worry continuously*) She frets away all the time when he isn't at home. Stop fretting away and expecting the worst!
- **frighten + particle** (*frighten, make afraid, with direction*) The noise frightened the children away. His

shotgun frightened off the birds. The gathering darkness frightened them in. Something frightened them out (of that house).
- **frisk + particle** (*move lightly and happily, with direction*) The young animals were frisking about. The children frisked in, yelling and singing.
- **fritter away** (*waste, spend in a stupid way*) She frittered away all her money. He has frittered away every chance he ever got.
- **frown (up)on** (*disapprove of, condemn*) He frowns upon things like that. Doesn't she frown upon that kind of behaviour? This is the kind of thing they frown on here.
- **fumble about/around** (*search about clumsily*) He fumbled about in his pocket for his keys. Stop fumbling around! What are you fumbling about for?
- **fuse together** 1 (*stick together, coalesce*) The metals fused together. 2 (*stick together, coalesce*) Can you fuse the two materials together? The metals had been fused together by the great heat.
- **fuss about/around** (*fuss generally, vaguely*) She fussed around all the time. Oh, stop fussing about and sit down!

G

- **gabble away** (*a*) (*jabber, chatter inarticulately and continuously*) The geese were gabbling away furiously. (*b*) (*talk away in a rowdy and rather incoherent manner*) The guests at the cocktail party were gabbling away.
- **gabble on** (*continue to gabble, like geese*) They gabbled on about their holiday plans till I could have screamed.
- **gad about/around** (*go about in a gay, light-hearted way*) He gads about without a care in the world. They gad

about a lot, going to expensive restaurants and shows. *noun* **a gadabout** = a person who gads about.

- **gain over** (*win over, convert*) They have gained him over. They expect to gain over a lot of converts.
- **gain (up)on** (*a*) (*catch up with, come closer to*) The horsemen were rapidly gaining on their enemy. Hurry up, they are gaining on us! (*b*) The company is gaining upon its rivals in volume of sales.
- **gallivant off** (*go off in a rather frivolous way*) She has gallivanted off somewhere with her friends.
- **gamble away** 1 (*gamble continuously*) They have been gambling away for days, almost forgetting to eat. 2 (*lose by gambling, forfeit*) He has gambled his whole fortune away. She has gambled away our chances of success.
- **gambol + particle** (*cavort and play, with direction*) The lambs were gambolling about in the fields. The children like to gambol around in the garden. The foal gambolled up aid took the sugar from my hand.
- **gather in** (collect as fully and closely as possible) The shepherd gathered in his sheep. The seamstress gathered in the cloth.
- **gather round** (*come together in a crowd*) Gather round, friends, and hear the news! The people gathered round, curious to know what was happening.
- **gather together** 2 (*bring together in a group*) He gathered the animals together. They gathered their belongings together, and set off. She gathered some friends together.
- **gather up** (*pick up into one bundle, collect*) She gathered up the children's toys. He gathered the books up and put them away.

- **gaze about/around** (*look about*) She gazed about at the strange landscape. He gazed about, trying to decide where the danger lay.
- **gaze away** (*a*) (*look continuously*) I love this painting, and could gaze away at it for hours. (*b*) (*gaze into the far distance*) She stands on the cliff and gazes away out to sea.
- **gaze out** (*took out*) The men were gazing out to sea. She stood at the window, gazing out.
- **gear up** (*a*) (*fit with gears*) The machine is now geared up and ready for use. (*b*) (*make ready*) The team is geared up, fit for anything. I hope you are all geared up for the new sales campaign. He geared himself up for the interview.
- **gen up** 1 (*provide oneself with fullest possible information*) He genned up on all the problems. 2 (*provide with fullest possible information*) The air force commander genned his men up for the mission. He's all genned up about what to do and when to do it. He's really genned up on this kind of machine.
- **gesture + particle** (*invite or order by means of gestures, with direction*) She gestured him over. He gestured them up to where he was standing. They were gestured back, so that they wouldn't be seen.
- **get about/around** (*a*) (*move or go about*) He gets about quite well, despite his rheumatism. She is getting about again after her illness. She really does get about! (*b*) (*spread*) The news got about that he was leaving. Bad news certainly gets about. The report has got about that you won't help us. It must not get about that he is ill.
- **get back at** (*gain revenge on*) I'll get, back at them somehow for this! He got back at her for spoiling his evening. She got back at him by showing me the letter.

- **get by** (*a*) (*pass*) Let me get by, please. Can I get by? (*b*) (*be tolerable, be passable*) This work will get by, but that's all. It may just get by. (*c*) (*manage*) She gets by on a remarkably small income. We get by somehow, but it's not easy.
- **get down to** (*start to work seriously on*) I really must get down to some study. She decided to get down to her French. When you get down to it, it isn't so difficult.
- **get forward** 1 (*move forward*) They got forward to the front line without any enemy response. 2 (*convey forward*) We got it forward on time.
- **get in** 1(*a*) (*come in, enter*) He got in before the rain started. The sun gets in through these windows. Water gets in through this crack in the wall. (*b*) (*interpose oneself*) He got in between the other two people. (*c*) (*be admitted*) The child got in (to the school) after a special test. I think he will get in without too much trouble. (*d*) (*get home*) She said she would get in late tonight. What time does he get in? (*e*) (*be elected*) Their candidate got in all right. The party expects to get in at the next election. 2 (*a*) (*bring in*) He got the chairs in from the garden before the rain started. The farmers have begun getting in the harvest. She went out to get the washing in. The company is trying to get in all its outstanding debts. The government gets the taxes in quite efficiently. (*b*) (*push or screw in*) I can't get this nail in. Can you get this rod in without tools? (*c*) (*put in the ground*) It's time to get the bulbs in. He has got his seeds in already. (*d*) (*bring in as a supply*) She has got the groceries in for the whole week. He has gone out to get the coal in. (*e*) (*summon in*) They have got the doctor in to look at the child. She got the electrician in to check the wiring. We must get a joiner in to fix this cupboard.

- **get into** (*a*) (*be affected by, or involved in*) He gets into a terrible rage if you just mention politics. Don't get into such a panic! These books have got into an awful mess. The children are always getting into trouble/mischief. (*b*) *Idiom*: to get into the habit of= to become used to doing.
- **get off with** (*start having an affair with*) He got off with that blonde. She got off with a millionaire.
- **get on for** (*come close to, draw near to*) He must be getting on for forty now. She's getting on for 35 if she's a day! That old fellow is getting on for 100. It's getting on for midnight, and we really ought to be going home.
- **get on to** (*a*) (*recognize, trace, find*) The police will get on to him very soon. (*b*) (*nag*) She's always getting on to me about something. (*c*) (*contact, get in touch with*) I'll get on to them straight away and find out what is happening. He'll get on to us if anything goes wrong. Get on to your consul and ask his advice.
- **get on with** (*continue, proceed with*) I expect you all to get on with your work while I'm away. Get on with it! This is quite enough work to be getting on with.
- **get out** 1 (*a*) (*leave*) They decided to get out while there was still time. I'd better get out before I'm thrown out. Get out! (*b*) (*escape*) The prisoners got out through that window. The cat has got out again. (*c*) (*leak out, become known*) The news has got out that you are leaving. Don't let it get out that he is coming. 2 (*a*) (*remove, urn with an effort*) He got the cork out by pulling hard. The dentist managed to get the tooth out. She couldn't get the stain out. (*b*) (*bring out, make ready*) I'll get the car out and we can be off. They got the horses out. She got a bed out for her unexpected guest. (*c*) (*manage to produce*) He was very embarrassed, but somehow he got the apology

out. She sometimes finds it difficult to get her words out. (*d*) (*publish*) We expect to get the next edition out on time. They got the book out quickly. (*e*) (*borrow from a library etc*) She got the book out for a fortnight. (*f*) (*prepare and present*) They managed to get the plans out on time. He has got out a very interesting scheme. The accountant got the balance sheets out. When will you get the accounts out? (*g*) (*solve, calculate successfully*) He managed to get that puzzle out. I can't get this sum out.

- **get out of** (*a*) (*leave*) He got out of the car. She got out of bed. (*b*) *Idiom*: to get out of the way= to move to one side, to stop interfering or obstructing. (*c*) *Idiom*: to get out of one's depth=to become involved in something beyond one's ability to handle it. *Example*: He got out of his depth in that financial argument, because the other fellow knew the facts. (*d*) (*avoid*) I can't get out of going to see them. I wish I could get out of it. He hoped to get out of doing the work.

- **get round** 1 (*a*) = get about/around (*b*) (*by-pass an obstacle*) The damaged trucks were in the way, but our driver got round somehow. It may take time, but we'll get round. 2 (*a*) (*revive, restore to consciousness*) The doctor got the man round quite quickly after the accident. (*b*) (*convert, persuade*) We should have very little difficulty getting him round to our way of thinking. They'll get her round, don't worry. 3 (*a*) (*evade, circumvent*) He is trying to get round paying his taxes. You just can't get round the regulations in this way. There is no getting round the need for money. (*b*) (*coax, persuade to help*) She is so good at getting round him that she'll get the money all right. That child can always get round you and get what it wants.

- **get round to** (*find time to do*) He says he'll get round to it next week. I just can't get round to it. I always wanted to write, but have never got round to it. Perhaps we'll get round to doing it some day.
- **get through with** (*finish completely, use with a feeling of relief*) He finally got through with the subject. I'll be glad to get through with this whole project.
- **get together** 1 (*meet, informally*) The family is getting together for the anniversary. Some of the lads get together at the pub once a week. We must get together and discuss this. *noun* **a get-together** = an informal meeting or gathering. 2 (*bring together, assemble*) He got them together to talk matters over. It is difficult to get them all together under one roof. He tried to get all his thoughts together.
- **get up to** (*a*) (*catch up with, come level with*) I had just got up to their boat when a strong wind hit us. (*b*) (*reach*) I've got up to page 110 in the book. (*c*) (*involve oneself in*) He has got up to some new mischief. I wonder what she'll get up to next?
- **gibber away** (*a*) (*jabber continuously*) The chimpanzees were gibbering away to each other. (*b*) (*chatter away like an ape*) He gibbered away about his crazy ideas.
- **gird up** (*a*) (*fix up with a belt*) He girded up his tunic. (*b*) (prepare for action) He girded himself up.
- **give away** (*a*) (*bestow*) He gave the money away. I have given the book away. (*b*) (*distribute*) She gave the money away to the poor. The guest gave away the prizes. (*c*) (*betray*) The soldier gave away the secrets when the enemy tortured him. She's not giving away anything he told her. *Noun* **a give away** = something which gives away a secret. *Example*: Her guilty expression was a real give-away.

- **give back** (*a*) (*restore*) He gave back everything he had taken. Give the book back to your brother! They gave the people back their freedom. Living here has given me back my health. (*b*) (*return, reflect*) This chamber gives back a marvellous echo. The mirrors gave back hundreds of parallel images.
- **give in** 1 (*yield, surrender*) I give in. If we can't continue with the struggle, we may as well give in now. 2 (*hand, put or bring in*) They gave in the documents as requested. Where do we give in our names?
- **give off** (*emit, serve as the source of*) The steel plates were giving off a great deal of heat. This rotting vegetation gives off a terrible smell.
- **give on to** (*lead on to, provide access to*) This door gives on to the courtyard.
- **give out** 1 (*a*) (*come to an end*) The supplies are beginning to give out. Her patience gave out long ago. Has the money given out at last? (*b*) (*stop functioning*) The engine gave out. (*c*) (*announce*) He gave out that they weren't coming. 2 (*a*) (*distribute*) The teacher gave out the books. He will give out the money soon. (*b*) (*announce*) He gave the news out in a grave voice.
- **give over** 1 (*stop doing something*) I wish she would give over for a bit. Do give over. 2 (*transfer, hand over*) They gave the building over for use as an office. It's been given over to a charity.
- **glance + particle** (*look quickly, with direction*) He glanced back to see if they were following. She glanced up from her work to see who had come in. He glanced in as he passed.
- **glance off** (*a*) (*strike lightly or in passing; strike and ricochet*) The bullets struck the steel armor and glanced off. The spear harmlessly glanced off.

- **glass in** (*cover in with glass*) The area has been completely glassed in. I like the glassed-in effect.
- **glass over** (*cover over with glass*) The space has been glassed over.
- **gleam out** (*shine suddenly and brightly*) A light gleamed out in the darkness. His torch gleamed out.
- **glide + particle** (*glide, move smoothly and swiftly, with direction*) The ship glided along swiftly. The snake glided away into the undergrowth. She glided up to me and offered me a drink.
- **glimmer out** (*shine or gleam out weakly*) A light glimmered out hardly affecting the darkness.
- **gloom about/around** (*go about dejectedly*) they have been glooming about for days, since they were told they couldn't go.
- **gloss over** (a) (cover over with a shiny layer) The surface has been beautifully glossed over. (b) (hide or obscure with plausible argument; seek to conceal by passing on to another subject) He glossed over the various points raised by his critics. You can't just gloss it over like that! He always glosses these things over.
- **glow away** (*shine continuously*) The light glowed away in the darkness, reassuring everyone.
- **glow on** (*continue to glow*) The fire glowed on for several hours after it had lost its heat.
- **glow out** (*glow suddenly and brightly*) An intense light glowed out from the window of the house.
- **glue dawn** (*stick down with glue*) They glued the wood down.
- **glue on** (*stick on with glue*) He glued the paper on.
- **glue together** (*stick together with glue*) She glued the papers together. The materials are all glued together.

- **gnaw away** 1 (*gnaw, chew continuously*) The dog gnawed away on the bone. 2 (*remove or deface by gnawing*) The rats have gnawed the boards away. Something has gnawed the surface away.
- **go + particle** (*go, with direction*) He went away. She went in. They went out. I shall go back.
- **go about/around with** (*keep company with*) (*a*) (*for friendship*) He goes about with a nice group of boys. (*b*) (*for courting*) She goes about with that boy. He's going about with a very pretty girl.
- **go across** (*specifically, cross, traverse*) They went across to the other side.
- **go after** (*try to win*) He is going after the championship. Why don't you go after her? They both went after the same job/girl/prize.
- **go ahead** (*a*) (*specifically, move steadily forward*) The ship went ahead against the enemy bombardment. (*b*) (*continue, proceed*) They went ahead and told us what had happened. Go ahead, tell me. (*c*) (*carry on, proceed*) She just went ahead and did it. Please don't go ahead with it till you've seen me again.
- **go along** (*work through something*) I check the spelling as I go along.
- **go along with** (*concur, agree with*) I can't go along with you in this matters He could go along with it most of the way, but not entirely. I go along with you all the way.
- **go at** (*a*) (*attack*) He went at him with an axe. (*b*) (*undertake vigorously*) You should see her go at the job. He went at it with a will.
- **go away** (*a*) (*specifically, depart*) They went away and did not return. (*b*) (*elope*) He went away with his friends wife. They went away together.
- **go below** (*go below decks*) The captain went below.

- **go (on) before** (*die*) We music remember those who have gone on before.
- **go beyond** (*die*) He has gone beyond.
- **go by** 1 (*specifically pass by*) They went by without stopping. 2 (*base a judgment on*) There is very little to go by. We can't go by looks alone. Don't go by what I say. To go by appearances, I would say all is not well. If we go by instructions then we must leave now you can never go by what he says.
- **go forth** (*a*) (*march or journey out*) The army went forth amid great cheering and applause. He went forth up or a journey to a far land. (*b*) (*be sent out*) the command went forth that all men of a certain age should be killed.
- **go forward** (*a*) (*advance*) The soldiers went forward at dawn. (*b*) (*be put forward*) The suggestion went forward to the committee.
- **go in** (*a*) (*begin, begin work*) What time does the school/theatre go in? (*b*) (*attack a special place*) The infantry went in. The bombers will go in soon. (*c*) (*go behind clouds*) The sun has gone in.
- **go in for** (*a*) (*enter for be a candidate for*) He has gone in for the civil service exams. She has gone in for the beauty competition. Are you going in for the three-legged race? (*b*) (*enjoy have as a bobby*) She goes in for badminton and tennis. He goes in for athletics. I go in for stamp collecting and judo. She doesn't go in for walking much. (*c*) (*become occupied or concerned with*) One day he may go in form politics. He goes in for biology. (*d*) (*like, enjoy*) We don't go in for that sort of thing here. Some people go in for football in a big way.
- **go together** (*a*) (*court, keep company*) That fellow and that girl go together. (*b*) (*harmonize*) The colours go together (very well). These people go together all

right. (c) (*entail each other*) These events go together. Such conditions always seem to go together. Medical symptoms of this kind often go together.
- **go towards** (*serve as a contribution for*) This money will go towards the rehabilitation of the refugees.
- **goad on** (*force on with a good, incite*) the driver goaded the oxen on. (*b*) He goaded his opponents on to attack him. Stop goading them on.
- **gobble away** (*a*) (*gobble, eat quickly in large pieces, continuously*) The men gobbled away until all the food was gone. (*b*) (*make a gobbling noise continuously*) The turkeys were gobbling away.
- **gobble down** (gobble or cram down, swallow quickly in large quantities) The turkeys were gobbling away.
- **gobble down** (*gobble or cram down, swallow quickly in large quantities*) He just gobbles his food down. The animal gobbled down everything it was given.
- **gobble up** (*a*) (*eat up greedily*) He gobbled up the food as though he had been starving for a month. (*b*) This project just gobbles up money.
- **goof off** (*shirk responsibility*) If you ask him to do anything, he will just goof off.
- **goof up** (*spoil*) I'm afraid I've goofed in up. He always goofs things up.
- **grab away** 1 (*make continuous grabbing movements*) The monkey kept grabbing away at the food. 2 (*snatch away violently*) He grabbed the toy away from his companion.
- **grade down** (*a*) (*put in a lower grade or position*) They have been graded down because of their physical condition. (*b*) downgrade.
- **grade up** (*intensive of* grate, *shred*) She grated up the cheese. Would you grate these vegetables up?

- **grind down** (*a*) (*reduce, to a powder, by grinding*) the stones have been slowly ground down. Rock that has been ground down by the elements becomes soil. She ground the nutmeg down into powder. (*b*) (*oppress, weaken*) The dictator ground the people down. Some people say that capitalists like to grind down the poor.
- **grind out** (*a*) (*produce through a grinding process*) The powder is ground out through this machinery and into these containers. (*b*) (*produce mechanically*) The tunes are ground out by this old barrel organ. (*c*) (*keep on playing badly*) The musicians ground out their favourite melodies until we were tired of them. (*d*) (*produce, churn out*) The public relations people keep grinding out more information about how wonderful their companies are, I wish they would stop grinding out the same old propaganda.
- **grind up** (*grind thoroughly*) the materials have been ground up into a fine powder. This machine grinds all the refuse up.
- **groan out** 1 (*emit a groan*) She groaned out in her sleep. The sick man groaned out in pain. 2 (*emit as a groan*) The exhausted man groaned out his complaints. They heard him groan out something about an enemy attack. She groaned out that she never had any luck.
- **grope + particle** (*search, feel blindly with direction*) She groped about in the dark for the matches. He groped up from the cellar to the top of the stairs. They groped along until they came to a door.
- **grow out** (*grow in an outward direction*) The plants are beginning to grow out towards the sun.
- **grow out** of 1 (*a*) (*become too big for*) He has grown out of all his clothes. (*b*) I have grown out of these childish habits. 2 to outgrow = (*i*) to grow quicker than (someone or something else). (*ii*) grow out of.

- **grow together** (*a*) (*come together while growing*) These bushes and creepers have slowly grown together. (*b*) (*come closer together as time passed*) the two of them have grown together over the years. We were not always such close friends, but have grown together during these difficult times.
- **grub about/around** (*search diligently about like a bird looking for grubs*) She was grubbing about for something in her handbag. Stop grubbing about there and tell me what you're looking for. He's been grubbing about for a job without success.
- **guide+particle** (*guide or conduct, with direction*) The usher guided us in. We were guided out without difficulty. A man on the far side of the river guided them over.
- **gulp back** (*restrain with an effort*) She gulped back her tears. He gulped back the furious reply he wanted to make.
- **gulp down** (*swallow greedily*) They gulped the water down. He gulped down his beer.
- **gum on** (*fix or put on with gum or glue*) He gummed on the stamp. She gummed the label (back) on after it came off.
- **gum up** (*a*) (*cover with gum or glue*) The works of the machine were gummed up with some kind of thick viscous material. (*b*) (*cause to slop, bring to a halt as f with gum or glue*) this has really gummed things up. All our plans are gummed up for want of capital.
- **gun down** (*shoot down with a gun*) The bandit gunned the guards down. I saw them gun down innocent women and children.
- **gurgle + particle** (*make a gurgling sound, with direction*) The little stream gurgled along through the woods. Water

was gurgling back up the waste-pipe. The liquid gurgled away.
- **gush + particle** (*gush, pour, with direction*) The water gushed away through the huge hole. Oil was gushing up out of the ground. Blood gushed out (of the wound).
- **guzzle away** (*eat or drink greedily, continuously*) They guzzle away like pigs whenever they get the chance.

H

- **hack down** (*cut down or fell, violently or unevenly*) He hacked down the undergrowth to clear a path. They hacked down several bushes out of sheer vandalism.
- **hack out** (*cut violently or unevenly*) The settlers hacked out a clearing in the wilderness where they would eventually build their homes.
- **hack up** (cut up violently or unevenly) The rioters hacked up the furniture in the embassy and smashed the windows.
- **hail down** 1 (*pour down fiercely*) Stones hailed down on them. 2 (*call down or summon*) The prophet hailed down curses on the heads of the men who would not heed him.
- **hammer down** (*a*) (*fix down with nails, by hammering*) He hammered the planks down. (*b*) (*shape by continuous hammering*) He hammered down the metal till it was the shape he wanted.
- **hammer in** (*a*) (*fix in by hammering*) He hammered in the nail. (*b*) (*knock in by heavy blows*) They hammered in the door and then charged into the room. (*c*) (*inculcate or emphasise by continuous hard effort*) I'll hammer some information in whether that child likes it or not.

He intends to hammer in the point that his men will not accept the offer.
- **hand up** (*Old help up by hand*) He handed her up into the carriage. *n* a hand-up. *Example*: If you give me a hand-up I can get over the wall all right.
- **hang about/around** (*remain idling in a place*) Those young fellows have been hanging about for hours. I wish he would stop hanging about and do something useful. You shouldn't keep these people hanging about waiting for you. He hung about, hoping to see someone he knew.
- **hang back** 1 (*hesitate*) She hang back from asking the questions. I don't know why he always hangs back when he gets the chance to do something. 2 (*restore to a hanging position*) They didn't need the clothes, so they hung them back in the wardrobe.
- **hang behind** (*lag behind, linger behind*) That child hangs behind everywhere we go. She was hanging behind, too shy to speak.
- **hang down** (*dangle down*) The rope hung down from the ceiling.
- **hang on** 1 (*a*) (*hold on, sometimes precariously*) The climber on the ledge hung on precariously, waiting for help. (*b*) (*wait*) Hang on till I get help. Hang on and I'll come with you. 2 (*a*) (*wait (up) on depend (up) on*) Everything hangs on his decision. It all hangs on whether he is willing to help us. (*b*) (*listen with fascination*) The girl hung on his every word.
- **hang on to** (*a*) (*hold on to*) She hung on to his arm. (*b*) (*retain, often with determination*) You should hang on to that painting, because it may be worth a lot of money.

- **hare + particle** (*move quickly, like a hare*) The animals were haring along. The boys hared out to see the new arrivals.
- **hark back** (*refer back*) He harked back to his youth. They are always harking back to their days in the army.
- **harp on** (*talk continually, moan*) He harps on about how he has been cheated. I wish you wouldn't harp on about it all the time.
- **hash over** (*discuss*) They hashed over all their old problems.
- **hash up** (*spoil*) He's hashed up our plans again.
- **hasten + particle** (*hurry, with direction*) They hastened away. She hastened back to meet us.
- **hatch out** 1 (*emerge from an egg*) The chicks have hatched out. 2 (*form, develop*) He has hatched out a new plan.
- **haul down** (*pull down violently or with some effort*) They hauled the material down from the shelf (*sailing*) The sailors hauled down the flag/sails.
- **haul up** (*a*) (*pull up violently or with some effort*) They hauled the materials up from the cellar. The sailors hauled up the flag/sails. The sailors hauled up the small boat on to the deck of the ship. The boat was hauled up on to the beach. (*b*) (*Sl: summon*) He has been hauled up before the magistrate on a charge of assault.
- **have at** (*attack*) Have at them! (*Fencing*) Have at you!
- **have down** (*entertain by invitation, often in the country*) We are having the Smiths down for a few days.
- **have in** (*a*) (*entertain in the home by invitation*) We are having the Smiths in for dinner tonight. (*b*) (*send for, summon*) I think we had better have the doctor in.

- **have on** (*a*) (*wear*) She had nothing on. He had on a raincoat and boots. (*b*) (*be engaged in doing*) He has a lot on at the moment, but should be free next week. I have nothing on (for) this evening. (*c*) (*deceive, tease, mislead*) I'm afraid he must have been having you on. Stop having us on, please!
- **have up** (*a*) (*bring, order or invite up from a lower place*) We had them up for coffee last night. I had him up to see me, to explain what he was doing. (*b*) (*summons*) He was had up (by the police) for dangerous driving.
- **head back** (*go back, return*) We changed our minds and headed back to London.
- **head for** (*a*) (*have as a destination*) The ship was heading for Southampton. The car was heading for Glasgow. The police expected the criminals to head for the coast. (*b*) You're heading for trouble if you go on behaving like that.
- **hew up** (*cut up forcefully*) They hewed up plenty of wood for their winter supply.
- **hide away** 1 (*conceal oneself*) The little girl hid away in the cellar. 2 (*conceal*) We hid the toys away in the attic, where the children would not find them. The villagers hid the smuggler away until the revenue men had gone.
- **hide out** (*conceal oneself for a period of time*) The outlaw hid out in the hills for months. The police knew that the wanted men were hiding out somewhere in the town. *noun* **a hideout**=a place to hide.
- **hire out** (*give out on hire, lend for payment*) The company hires out cars. They hire out machinery for this kind of work.
- **hit back** 1 (*resist actively*) We must hit back against this tyranny. He hit back at his opponents in the debate. 2 (*strike in return*) The little boy hit the big boy back.

- **hit off** (*a*) (*achieve, mainly in imitation*) He hit off a perfect likeness when he drew his friend's face. He imitates voices, and can hit off some famous people beautifully. (*b*) (*be friendly*) He hit it off with them from the start.

- **hit out** (*a*) (*attack violently, and often without skill*) He began to hit out despairingly at his attackers. (*b*) The men are angry and ready to hit out in almost any direction. The MP hit out at Government policy on unemployment.

- **hit (up)on** (*find, discover*) He hit upon the solution to the problem almost by accident. I hope someone hits on a way out of this difficulty soon.

- **hitch up** (*a*) (*harness*) The farmer hitched up the horses to the cart. The men hitched the oxen up and started the long, slow journey in the wagons. (*b*) (*Lift into proper position*) He hitched up his trousers, which were rather loose.

- **hoard up** (*gather in a hoard, preserve for the future*) The old man must have hoarded up a lot of money over the years. They don't spend much, so I suppose they just hoard it all up.

- **hobble + particle** (*walk or move with short difficult steps, with direction*) The old man hobbled along, leaning on his stick. The injured men hobbled over to the emergency centre. The lame horse hobbled over to the emergency centre. The lame horse hobbled up.

- **hoist + particle** (*lift, by some contrivance, with direction*) They tried to hoist the huge stones up with a rope, but failed. The dockside cranes soon hoisted the cargo off.

- **hold by** (*adhere to; accept*) I don't hold by such foolish ideas.

- **hold down** (*a*) (*keep on the ground or in place*) They held the man down, to prevent him escaping. It was necessary

to hold the tents down because of the strong wind. (*b*) (*have*) He holds down quite a good job in the city.
- **hold forth** 1 (*perorate, make a speech*) The chairman held forth for several minutes on the dangers of indecision. 2 (*offer*) The management holds forth the prospect of rapid promotion to young men with enthusiasm and initiative.
- **hold in** (*a*) (*restrain*) The rider held in his horse, although it clearly wanted to gallop. (*b*) (*restrain, suppress*) She is very good at holding in her emotions.
- **hold out** 1 (*a*) (*continue, last*) How long will our food supply hold out? (*b*) (*continue to resist*) The battalion held out for a week in the face of heavy enemy assaults. (*c*) (*maintain a negotiating position*) The trade union intends to hold out for better pay and conditions. 2 (*a*) (*extend*) She held out her arms to embrace the little girl. (*b*) (*offer*) I'm afraid that his case holds out very little hope.
- **hold out on** (*keep something secret from*) He must know more than he will admit—I think he's holding out on us.
- **hold over** (*postpone, delay*) The meeting was held over until Friday.
- **hold to** (*adhere*) I hold to everything I said at the meeting. He has always held to his religious beliefs very firmly.
- **hold together** 1 (*remain in one piece, remain united*) This old coat hardly holds together any more. I expect the family to hold together in an emergency like this. 2 (*a*) (*keep together with the hands*) He held the wires together while his companion fitted them into place. (*b*) (*keep united*) He hopes to hold the family together through this difficult period.
- **hold with** (*approve of, condone*) I do not hold with heavy drinking and wild parties.

- **hole out** (*to hit the ball into a hole*) He holed out in four, one under par.
- **hole up** (*hide, conceal oneself*) The thieves holed up in a mountain hut after their escape from the police.
- **hollow out** (*make a hollow or cavity*) The animal hollowed out a place for itself and lay down. The men hollowed out a tree-trunk in order to make a canoe.
- **hop off** (*a*) (*go away hurriedly*) He just hopped off without telling us he was going.
- **horn in** (*join in, without invitation, like an animal using its horns*) Those gangsters just horned in on legitimate business in the state and started running things.
- **horseabout/around** (*behave in an animals, rather rough way, said of young people*) The boys were horsing about in the back garden, making a lot of noise and getting dirty.
- **hose down** (*clean down with water from a hose*) They hosed down the cars and then polished them.
- **hose out** (clean down with water from a hose) He hosed out the stable.
- **hot up** 1 (*a*) (heat up) (*become hot*) The soup soon began hotting up. (*b*) (*become dangerous*) Things are beginning to hot up in the Middle East again. (*c*) (*become fast or more exciting*) The music began to hot up. The pace of the investigation began to hot up, as the police closed in on the criminals. 2 (*make hot*) She said she would hot up some soup.
- **hound out** (*hunt out, as with dogs*) They are determined to hound out law-breakers.
- **hover about/around** (*a*) (*hover in the area*) Many little birds were hovering about. (*b*) (*wait around in an apparently aimless way*) That fellow has been hovering

about here for several days, and I would like to know what he wants.
- **howl away** (*howl continuously*) The wolves have been howling away on the edge of the forest for hours.
- **howl out** (*cry in a sudden and loud manner*) The man howled out in pain. 2 They howled out their hatred.
- **hunch up** (*form into a hunch or hump*) He hunched up his shoulders against the cold, driving rain. The figure was hunched up in a corner of the room.
- **hunt after/for** (*seek, look for*) The men had been hunting after that animal for weeks, without success. She was hunting after a particular king of coat and finally found it.
- **hunt down** (*hunt with determination*) The men hunted down the mad dog until they cornered and shot it. The police were intent upon hunting down the escaped convict.
- **huddle away** (*crowd together out of sight*) The children huddled away in a corner.
- **huddle down** (*intensive of* huddle) The child huddled down in the bed, listening to the sound of the storm.
- **huddle together** The animals huddled together for warmth.
- **huddle up** (*gather in a tight group*) The refugees huddled up in one part of the house, frightened and uncertain.
- **hurl + particle** (*throw violently or with great effort, with direction*) The men hurled the rocks down on their attackers. He picked up a stone and hurled it out of the window.
- **hurry + particle** 1 (*move quickly with direction*) The people hurried along. They hurried in. Please hurry up! 2 The guards hurried the prisoners up. The scorn hurried the men out.

- **hurtle + particle** (*move at very at very great speed, with direction*) The train hurtled along at 120 mph. The rocket hurtled upwards towards the moon. The meteorite hurtled downwards and struck the earth.
- hush up 1 (*be quiet*) Oh, do hush up! 2 (*suppress*) They tried to hush up the scandal, but news soon leaked out. The politicians hushed the whole affair up.
- **hustle + particle** (*move in a quick, busy fashion*) The men were hustled along by their guide. An eager official hustled us out after our meeting with the famous man.

I

- **ice in** (*enclose or surround with ice*) We can't move the machinery, because it is iced in.
- **ice over** (*become covered with ice*) The weather has turned very cold and the lake has iced over. The windows of the car are icing over.
- **ice up** 1 (*become completely covered with or full of ice*) The wings of the aircraft have iced up. The car windscreen is beginning to ice up. 2 The water pipes are all iced up.
- **idle about/around** (*move about in an lazy way*) I asked him to stop idling about and do something useful.
- **idle away** 1 (*operate continuously, while disengaged*) The car engine has been idling away for several minutes, to get it warm. 2 (*waste*) He has been idling his time away on the beach, lying around and doing nothing.
- **ink in** (*fill in, using ink*) She inked in the outlines on the paper. He did the outline work and then she inked the rest of the drawing in.
- **ink out** (*delete, using ink*) He inked out the mistakes in the typescript.

- **ink over** (*go over with a pen*) You must ink over your signature, pencil writing is not allowed.
- **inquire after** (*ask for information about*) They have been inquiring after houses in this neighbourhood. He inquired after your health. They were inquiring after a Mr. Smith but I knew nothing about him.
- **inquire into** (*investigate*) The police decided to inquire into the events leading up to the accident. I expect that you will want to inquire into the reasons for this decision.
- **iron out** (*a*) (*smooth, using a hot iron*) She ironed out all the creases in the shirt. (*b*) (*smooth, as if using a hot iron; resolve*) He expects to iron out these difficulties at a special conference next week. They are experts at ironing out the problems that arise at international gatherings.
- **issue forth** (*emerge, pour forth or out*) The soldiers issued forth from a side gate in the wall, and attacked their besiegers. A stream of foul language issued forth from her lips.

J

- **jab + particle** 1 (*stick or poke, with direction*) The boy jabbed the stick in. 2 (*move by means of jabbing or poking, with direction*) He jabbed the beetle out with a stick.
- **jabber away** (*talk repetitious nonsense*) The monkey jabbered away in a corner. I'm tired of these politicians jabbering away about matters of which they have no knowledge.
- **jabber out** (*jabber cloud; say so rapidly as to reduce to nonsense*) She jabbered out her prayers, to finish them as quickly as possible.

- **jack in** (*conclude, stop, with a suggestion of irritation or frustration*) It's time we jacked this work in. I've had enough I'm going to jack it in now.
- **jack up** (*a*) (*raise by means of a jack*) He jacked up the wheel of the car, in order to repair the puncture. (*b*) (*raise, increase*) Prices have been jacked up a lot this year.
- **jam + particle** (*push hard, with direction*) He jammed the stick through until it appeared on the other side of the wall. He jammed his hat on and went out. He jammed the material in until the cavity was full.
- **jam in** (*be caught in a jam, be unable to move in any direction*) My car has been jammed in by several lorries, and I can't get it out.
- **jam on** (*apply firmly*) The driver jammed on his brakes, to prevent an accident.
- **jar (up) on** (*have a harsh impact on*) This noise jars on my ears. Her constant complaining jars upon my nerves.
- **jaunt about/around** (*move around nonchalantly, casually*) They jaunt about quite a lot, especially during the summer. He spends a lot of time jaunting about on the continent.
- **jaw away** (*talk continuously, as if using the jaw too much*) I got tired of him jawing away all the time.
- **jazz up** (*a*) (*express as a form of jazz music*) They have begun jazzing up the Classics now. I wish they wouldn't jazz up all the old traditional tunes. (*b*) (*Make more exciting, revitalise*) The boys want to jazz up the house, change the decor, have brighter colours. (*c*) (*improve, give an appearance of improvement*) I've tried to jazz up the old car with a spot of paint and some accessories.

- **jib at** (*refuse to accept, reject*) The horse jibbed at that high fence. I jib at providing all this information in order to that I'm creditworthy.
- **jig + particle** (*move as though doing a lively dance, with direction*) The girls were jigging about in the living-room, all very excited. The little boy ran along, jigging in and out through the crowd.
- **jockey about/around** (*a*) (*move in order to achieve a desired position*) The men on the horses were jockeying about to get into a proper line. (*b*) The politicians jockeyed about in order to establish relative power within the party.
- **jog + particle** (*move at a slow steady run, with direction*) The athletes were jogging along. To get fit, he jogs up and down in the park almost every evening.
- **join in** 1 (*take part, participate*) you will be expected to join in at club parties. 2 He joined in the children's game, I invited her to join in the conversation. They joined in the general protest.
- **join on** 1 (*attach oneself to*) The people were hurrying to see the parade, and we joined on at the rear. 2 (*attach*) They joined the wires on and made the necessary new connection.
- **join up** 1 (*offer oneself as a recruit, sign on*) He has joined up in the Parachute Regiment. 2 (*connect, link together*) The electrician joined the wires up.
- **jolly along** (*encourage to move more quickly*) Would you jolly those people along a bit, please?
- **jolly up** (*encourage or cause to be more active*) It's time we jollied those people up and got the work done.
- **jostle + particle** (*move within a crowd, with direction*) They jostled through to the exit. The people were jostling along towards the city square.

- **jot down** (*write down in a short quick note*) He jotted down our telephone number.
- **journey + particle** (*travel, with direction*) They journeyed along through the wine country. We journeyed up from the coast at a leisurely pace.
- **jump + particle** (*jump, with direction*) The little boy was jumping up and down. The bus stopped and he jumped off. The train stopped and I jumped on.
- **jump at** (*accept with enthusiasm*) The said he would jump at the chance of going abroad. She jumped at the offer of a job.
- **jump on** (*criticise sharply or suddenly*) I told her what I had thought of doing, and she just jumped on me and said it was ridiculous.
- **jut out** (*protrude, stick out*) The stones jut out from the side of the building. His teeth tend to jut out a little.

K

- **keel over** (*capsize, begin to capsize*) The boat keeled over.
- **keep + particle** 1 (*remain with direction*) The police warned the people to keep away. We were asked to keep back from the entrance to the house. Keep down or the bullets will hit you! Danger, keep off! 2 (*keep with direction*) They kept us out. She kept the boy in. Would you keep that dog away, please?
- **keep at** (*a*) (*persist with*) He kept at the job till finished. Keep at it! (*b*) (*maintain pressure on*) Keep at him till he pays you.
- **keep away** (*abstain*) He keeps away from liquor and tobacco.

- **keep back** 1 (*a*) (*with hold*) National Insurance keeps back 5% of my wages. They are keeping back the names of the victims. (*b*) (*have as a secret, conceal*) You are keeping something back from us. (*c*) (*hinder*) I don't want to keep you back (from your work).
- **keep form** (*refrain, abstain from*) He keeps from alcohol. I hope you will keep from doing anything rash.
- **keep in** 1 (*stay friendly, try to stay in favour*) I'm trying to keep in with them. You should keep in with him as he is very influential. 2 (*a*) (*restrain*) He tries to keep his emotions in. (*b*) (*restrict to a place*) The teacher has decided to keep them in all afternoon, as a punishment for bad behaviour. (*c*) (*hold or pull in*) Keep your stomach in!
- **keep on** (*a*) (*continue*) He kept on till the work was finished. (*b*) (*continue to move*) The soldiers kept on towards their objective. 2 (*a*)
- **keep on about** (*keep talking irritatingly about*) She always keeps -on about the post of living.
- **keep on at** (*nag*) I wish you wouldn't keep on at me the whole time.
- **keep out** (*a*) (*maintain or have outside*) They keep the dog out most of the time. (*b*) (*provide insulation against*) That coat should keep out the cold.
- **keep out of** (*not become involved in*) You should keep out of these things. Keep out of what doesn't concern you.
- **keep to** (*a*) (*adhere to*) He always keeps to his promises. (*b*) (*stay in*) He has decided to keep to his bed.
- **keep together** (*maintain unity as a group*) He hopes to keep the family together.
- **kick away** 1 (*kick continuously*) The little boy was kicking away at the woodwork. 2 (*a*) (*remove as a*

support, by kicking) they kicked away the wooden posts and brought the whole thing down.
- **kick back** 1 (*recoil*) The engine kicked back. 2 (*a*) *Idiomatic*: *noun* **a kickback**=a cut or share in some deal, illegal.
- **kick in** (*knock or break in by kicking*) The attackers kicked the door in. The thugs kicked his teeth in.
- **kick off** 1 (*a*) (*begin the game by kicking the ball*) They kicked off bang on time. *noun* **the kick-off**=the start of a game. (*b*) (*begin, start*) When should we kick off? The party kicked off in great style.
- **kick out** 1 (*strike out with the foot or with hoofs*) The horse kicked out at them. 2 (*expel*) If I were you, I would kick those people out (of the house).
- **kick up** (*a*) (*cause*) The boys were kicking up a terrific row. She kicked up a fuss because we didn't go.
- **kid on** (*tease*) Stop kidding us all on.

L

- **ladle out** (*a*) (*serve with a large spoon*) She ladled out the soup. (*b*) He likes to ladle out advice.
- **lag behind** (*dawdle or linger behind*) The girls lagged behind, picking flowers. Some members of the convoy were beginning to lag behind.
- **lam into** (*a*) (*attack*) The boxer lamed into his opponent. (*b*) She lamed in to me about the mistake I had made.
- **land up** (*end up, finish*) He landed up in New York. Be careful or you'll land up in jail. He landed up sacked from the job after all.
- **lap over** (overlap, sit one partly on another) The tiles lap over.

- **lap up** (*a*) (*scoop up with the tongue*) The cat lapped up the milk. (*b*) (*enjoy, accept happily*) He just laps up flattery. They lapped up the special treatment given them.
- **lark about/around** (*play or romp about, in a rather noisy manner*) The boys were larking about on the street corner.
- **lash about/around** (*move or thrash about violently*) the animal lashed about in pain. The prisoner lashed about, but could not break his bonds.
- **lash down** 1 (*fall violently*) The rain was lashing down. 2 (*tie down tightly with ropes*) The cargo was lashed down on the deck of the ship.
- **lash out** (*a*) (*attack*) He lashed out at the burglar with a stick. (*b*) The politicians lashed out at the opposition policy. (*c*) (*spend lavishly*) Her father has really lashed out on her education.
- **lash up** (*tie up tightly with ropes*) the equipment is lashed up and ready to go.
- **last out** 1 (*Endure, Survive*) I think they will last out till they are rescued. 2 (*survive*) I don't think the old man will last out the winter.
- **latch on** (*a*) (*seize hold*) The dog latched on and wouldn't let go. (*b*) (*understand*) I don't think he has latched on to what we are doing. She just hasn't latched on.
- **latch on to** (*acquire*) He has latched on to some very valuable pieces of property.
- **laugh at** (*a*) (*get amused about*) What are you laughing at? That is nothing to laugh at. (*b*) (*mock*) She was laughing at us all the time. (*c*) (*dismiss as unimportant*) They laughed at the idea.
- **laugh away** 1 (*laugh continuously*) He was laughing away to himself all the time 2 (*dismiss with laughter, scorn*) He laughed away the dangers.

- **laugh down** (*defeat, dismiss or silence by laughing*) The audience laughed the speaker down.
- **launch forth** 1 (*begin with vigour or drama*) He launched forth into a colourful description of his journey. 2 (*send out with great vigour or display*) This party should launch them forth into society.
- **launch out** (*start vigorously*) He has launched out into a new line of business.
- **lay + particle** (*put or place, with direction*) He laid the box down. She laid the book aside for a moment. They laid the materials back in the cupboard.
- **lay about** 1 (*strike violently*) He laid about with a stick. 2 (*attack violently*) He laid about them with a stick.
- **lay alongside** (*place beside*) They brought the ship up to the others and laid her alongside.
- **lay aside** (*abandon*) I want you to lay aside these useless prejudices. He laid aside his scruples and joined the gang.
- **lay by** (*same*) The old woman had laid by a little money.
- **lever out** (*a*) (*remove by means of a lever*) He levered the stone out. (*b*) They have tried to lever him out of his powerful position. (*c*) (*lift out*) He levered himself out of the chair.
- **lever up** (*raise by means of a lever*) They managed to lever up the stone slab and look underneath.
- **lick off** (remove by licking with the tongue) She licked the cream off.
- **lick up** (*lift by licking*) The dog licked up the gravy.
- **lie back** (*a*) (*recline*) He lay back in the comfortable chair. She lay back in bed. (*b*) Just lie back and enjoy yourself here.

- **lie in** (*a*) (*stay in bed*) He is lying in this morning. *noun* **a lie-in**. (*b*) (*be confined for childbirth*) She is lying in. *noun* **a lying-in hospital** = a maternity hospital.
- **lie off** (*rest nearby*) The ship is now lying off, ready to load up.
- **lie over** (*be postponed, be adjourned*) The decision must lie over until the next executive meeting.
- **lie to** (*a*) (*be moored, anchored*) The ship was lying to outside the harbour. (*b*) (*come into position for anchoring*) The ship lay to.
- **lie up** (*a*) (*rest*) He intends to lie up for a time. (*b*) (*remain in hiding*) The criminals are lying up somewhere in those hills. (*c*) (*be out of use*). My car has been lying up all winter.
- **lift down** (*lift and then bring down*) He lifted the books down from the top shelf.
- **lift off** 1 (*leave the ground*) The heavy bombers slowly lifted off. The rocket lifted off from its launching pad. 2 (*raise and remove*) He lifted off the lid of the pot.
- **listen in** (*listen on a radio receiver or telephone*) We listened in to some very interesting programmes last night. Someone has been listening in to our telephone conversation. *noun* **a listener-in.**
- **loll back** (*lie back, in a lazy and slovenly manner*) The men lolled back in their armchairs, drinking beer.
- **look out** 1 (*a*) (*take care, be careful*) Look out! (*b*) (*keep watch*) **look out for** (*c*) *noun* **a look-out** = soldier, person, on watch. *noun* **a look-out post/station/tower**. 2 (*search for*) I'll look out the photographs you want to see. 3 *Idiomatic warning*: It's your lookout=It will be your problem. 4 *noun* **outlook**=future state of the weather/one's career etc. *Example:* I'm afraid the outlook for tomorrow is rather grim.

- **look out for** (*a*) (*seek*) I'm looking out for a new house. (*b*) (*keep a watch for*) I want you to look out for them at the meeting. *Idiom*: keep a sharp look out= (*i*) observe everything carefully. (*ii*) watch carefully what you are doing.
- **look round** (*visit, inspect, tour*) The party was looking round the factory. We want to look round the town.
- **look to** (*a*) (*take care of*) Would you look to the children, please. (*b*) (*rely on*) I look to my parents when I need help.
- **look up** 1 (*improve*) The weather is looking up. His prospects in life seem to be looking up. Business is looking up. Things are looking up now. 2 (*a*) (*go to visit*) I want to look them up sometime. (*b*) (*seek, search for, look for*) I shall look up their number in the telephone directory. He looked the word up in the dictionary.
- **look (up)on** (*regard, view, consider*) We look upon these people as our most dangerous rivals. I shall look upon your son favourably when he comes.
- **look up to** (*admire, respect*) I really look up to him.
- **loom up** (*appear ominously*) The ship loomed up out of the fog.
- **loop back** 1 (*return in a loop or circle*) The wires loop back at this point. 2 (*take back in a loop*) He looped the wires back.
- **loosen up** 1 (*become loose, relax*) (*a*) This rope has loosened up. My muscles have begun to loosen up again. (*b*) The government has considerably loosened up on taxation. 2 (*loosen as much as possible*) He has loosened the soil up with a fork.
- **lop off** (*cut off quickly*) They lopped a lot of old branches off. The soldiers lopped off their prisoners' heads.

- **lose out** (*lose badly*) I think we have lost out. We certainly lost out on that deal.
- **lump together** (*take together as a lump*) He has lumped everyone together. We don't want to be lumped together in one group.

M

- **make after** (*pursue*) They made after him on horseback.
- **make at** (*attack*) He made at her with a knife.
- **make away with** (*murder secretly*) They made away with their opponents.
- **make for** (*a*) (*go towards, as a destination*) The party was making for London. The ship made for Southampton. (*b*) (*have a result, provide basis for*) This kind of thing makes for good human relations.
- **make off** (*escape*) When the police arrived, the thieves made off.
- **make off with** (*steal, decamp with*) The manager has made off with the company profits.
- **make over** (*a*) (*assign*) He has made the estate over to his eldest son. He has made the money over to charity. (*b*) (*remake*) She has made the coat over and it looks quite fashionable now.
- **make up for** (*compensate for*) He tried to make tip for all the trouble/worry he had caused.
- **make up to** (*flatter*) She makes up to her boss all the time.
- **mangle up** (*crush thoroughly*) The bodies of the accident victims were all mangled up.

- **manipulate + particle** (*arrange at will, with direction*) They manipulated the parts up into place. We may manage to manipulate the pieces out. I don't like people who try to manipulate you about to suit themselves.
- **map out** (*a*) (*mark out on a map*) The scouts mapped the area out thoroughly. (*b*) (*plan*) We have mapped out a plan of campaign. He has mapped out what he will do.
- **march past** (*a*) (*go past in ceremonial formation*) The contingents of the army, navy and air force marched past. *noun* **a march past**.
- **mark down** (*a*) (*note down with a mark*) Would you mark these points down? (*b*) (*reduce in price*) All these items have been marked down. (*c*) (*single out*) He has been marked down for assassination. They marked him down for promotion.
- **mans on** (*put on with a mark*) They have marked the prices on.
- **mark off** (*delimit indicate the boundaries by marking*) This area has been marked off for athletic practice.
- **mark out** (*a*) (*delineate*) The tennis court has been freshly marked out. (*b*) (*indicate*) They have marked out exactly what they intend to do. (*c*) (*note*) He has been marked out for early promotion.
- **mark up** (*a*) (*put up with a mark*) They marked up the score on the scoreboard. (*b*) (*put a price on*) They have marked up all these items. (*c*) (*raise in price*) These items have now been marked up.
- **marry off** (*arrange the marriage of*) He has married off his daughter to a rich young lawyer. They couldn't marry her off.
- **mash up** (*mash thoroughly, reduce to a pulp*) (*a*) The potatoes have been mashed up. (*b*) His face was mashed tip in the accident.

- **match up** 1 (*a*) (*correspond*) These colours match up nicely. (*b*) (*be equal*) He matched up to the situation. 2 (*bring into correspondence or harmony*) She has matched the patterns up very well.
- **meander + particle** (*move slowly and erratically, with direction*) The river meandered along. The party of pilgrims meandered back and forward in the temple grounds.
- **measure off** (*delimit or mark off by measuring*) They measured off the area in which they would work.
- **mete out** (*apportion, dispense*) The judge meted out punishment impartially. It is not my intention to mete out praise or blame.
- **mill about/around** (*crowd about in confusion*) The frightened animals were milling about in their pens. The people in the streets milled about.
- **mince + particle** (*walk or move in an affected or effeminate way, with direction*) The dandies minced along in their most colourful clothes. A young fop minced up and introduced himself.
- **mince up** (*reduce to mince*) The butcher minced the meat up.
- **mind out** (*take care*) Mind out or you'll get hurt!
- **miss out** 1 (*miss completely, lose*) I'm afraid I missed out on that deal. 2 (*omit*) We missed your name out by mistake. They decided to miss out the last part of the play.
- **mist over** (*become misty*) The windscreen of the car misted over.
- **mist up** (*make misty*) The condensation has begun to mist up the windows.

- **mix in** 1 (*take part in things*) She doesn't mix in very well. 2 (*add by mixing*) She mixed in the eggs. He carefully mixed the powder in.
- **mix round** (*stir and mix*) He mixed round the contents of the pot.
- **mix together** 1 (*mingle*) The people mixed together amicably. 2 (*put together by mixing*) You should mix the ingredients together.
- **mock-up** *noun* (*a scale model*) They made a mock-up of the campaign. The architect showed a mock-up of his plans.
- **monkey about/around** (*act like a monkey or foolishly*) Those boys have been monkeying about with my tools again. Stop monkeying about!
- **mooch + particle** (*move in an aimless, sullen, slovenly manner, with direction*) The disgruntled boys mooched off. He mooched along with his hands in his pockets. Those fellows have been mooching around here too much.
- **moon about/around** (*go about in a listless manner*) She has been mooning about all day, thinking about her boy friend.
- **mop down** (*clean down with a mop*) She mopped the walls down.
- **mop over** (*clean over with a mop*) She mopped over the floors.
- **mop up** 1 (*clean up with a mop*) Don't worry about the mess; I'll mop it up. 2 (*a*) (*clean up with a mop*) He mopped up the water. (*b*) (*eliminate*) The army has now mopped up the enemy. **mopping-up operations** = operations for ending enemy resistance.

- **mosey along/on** (*go informally along*) I guess I'd better mosey along out of here.
- **motor + particle** (*travel by car, with direction*) He is motoring down to the coast. They intend to motor up to London. Oh, he motored off somewhere for the weekend.
- **mount up** (*increase*) His debts are beginning to mount up.
- **move about/around** 1 (*a*) (*travel about*) They moved about a lot. (*b*) (*fidget*) The children kept moving about.
- **move along** (*policeman's order*) Move along now! Move along there, please!
- **move away** (*leave an area or a house*) They moved away a year ago.
- **move out** (*quit, leave*) The company has moved out. Our neighbors are moving out.
- **move up** 1 (*rise in rank*) He is moving up. 2 (*promote*) They are moving him up.
- **mow down** (*kill quickly in large numbers*) The machine-guns mowed down the advancing lines of infantrymen.
- **muck about/around** (*a*) (*do aimless things*) The boys were mucking about in their room. Stop mucking about (*b*) (*meddle*) He keeps mucking about with things he doesn't understand. (*c*) (*tinker for amusement*) I'm just mucking about with this old watch. 2 (*irritate*) He seems to enjoy mucking me about. Stop mucking us about!
- **muck in** (*take part*) Come on, muck in! Everyone mucks in here.
- **muck out** (*clean thoroughly*) They mucked out the stables.
- **muck up** (*a*) (*make dirty*) The children have mucked the whole place up. (*b*) (*spoil*) They have mucked my plans up completely.
- **muddle along** (*manage somehow*) Oh, we muddle along, you know, though we're not rich.

- **muddle on** (*continue to muddle, manage*) They muddle on in their own way.
- **muddle through** (*survive or win somehow*) We'll muddle through, don't worry.
- **muddle up** (*mix up, confuse*) Their names have been muddled up. I'm feeling rather muddled up. Don't muddle me up.
- **muffle up** 1 (*cover up fully*) Make sure you muffle up properly, because it's pretty cold outside. 2 (*muffle up completely; silence or reduce by muffling*) They muffled up the noise with blankets. His voice sounded muffled up.
- **mug up** (*learn thoroughly, for an exam*) He has been mugging up his Latin.
- **mull over** (*think over, consider carefully*) He mulled the idea over in his mind.
- **mumble away** (*speak indistinctly and continuously*) The old man mumbled away to himself. She was mumbling away about her problems.
- **munch up** (*chew up vigorously*) He munched up the celery.

N

- **nag away/on** (*nag continuously*) She has been nagging away at him for years.
- **nail down** (*a*) (*fix down with nails*) He nailed the lid down. (*b*) (*make agree*) I nailed him down to coming at six. (*c*) (*force to take a firm position*). We will eventually nail you down on this point.
- **nail up** (*a*) (*fix up with nails*) He nailed the picture up (on the wall). (*b*) (*seal with nails*) He nailed the door up. He nailed the goods up in a crate.

- **natter away** (*talk or chatter away amiably*) The two of them often natter away for hours.
- **navigate + particle** 1 (*steer, guide, with, direction*) He navigated out of the channel. They navigated through successfully. 2 He navigated the ship out of the channel. They navigated the boat through successfully.
- **need + particle** (*need, with direction*) I need her over to help me with the children. I need this tooth out. Do you need the book back tomorrow?
- **nestle down** (*snuggle down comfortably*) The children nestled down in their beds.
- **nestle in** (*snuggle in comfortably*) The animals nestled in against their mother.
- **nestle up** (*snuggle affectionately close*) She nestled up to him. He nestled up as close as he could get.
- **nibble away** 1 (*nibble by eating in small pieces continuously*) That child is always nibbling away at something. 2 (*remove by nibbling*) (*a*) The mice have nibbled away the edges of these papers. (*b*) Neighbouring countries have been nibbling territory away for years.
- **nibble off** (*cut off or separate by nibbling*) The rats have nibbled the tops off and left the rest.
- **nick in** (*slip suddenly in front of*) The car nicked in ahead of the lorry and almost caused an accident.
- **nip + particle** (*move very quickly, with direction*) They nipped off without telling us where they were going. Nip up and tell him to come down for his breakfast. They are constantly nipping in and out of each other's houses.
- **nip away** (*remove by nipping or pinching*) He nipped away the ends with a pair of pliers.
- **nip off** (*cut off with a nipping action*) You should nip off the flowers so that the rest of the plant can grow more vigorously.

- **nip out** (*take out or remove fully by a nipping action*) You should nip these weeds out before they become a real nuisance.
- **nod off** (*begin to fall asleep*) The old man was nodding off by the fire.
- **noise about/around/abroad** (*spread around as news*) They have noised the agreement about already, without waiting for permission.
- **nose + particle** 1 (*investigate, as f with the nose, with direction*) They have been nosing about here again. I don't like those men nosing in and out all day, asking questions. 2 (*bring or drive nose first, with direction*) He nosed the car out into the road. She carefully nosed the vacuum cleaner into all the corners.
- **number off** 1 (*mark off by numbers or in sequence*) The soldiers numbered off from the right. 2 The sergeant numbered his men off from the right.
- **nurse through** (*assist to survive or to get better by nursing*) (*a*) She nursed him through. (*b*) hope you will help to nurse this project through.
- **nuzzle in** (*become comfortable by small wriggling actions*) The children nuzzled in under the blankets.
- **nuzzle up** (*become close and comfortable by small wriggling actions*) The children nuzzled up against their sleeping mother.

O

- **offer up** (*offer to a superior person or power*) They offered up sacrifices once a year to the gods. The priest offered up prayers of thanksgiving to God. I suppose he expects us to offer up praise and adoration to him because he's our boss.

- **oil over** (*cover completely with oil*) He oiled the tools over and put them away in the shed. The athlete oiled himself over.
- **ooze + particle** (*move out slowly, said of liquids, with direction*) The oil began to ooze out through the tiny hole. I imagine the flood waters will ooze away over the next few days. His enthusiasm slowly began to ooze away in the face of their hostility.
- **open out** 1 (*a*) (*open wide*) The flower opened out when the sun came out. (*b*) (*become less shy*) The young girl began to open out once we had got to know her better. (*c*) (*spread as a panorama*) The countryside opens out beyond those trees, and you can see for miles. 2 (*unfold*) He opened out the map and studied our position.
- **open up** 1 (*a*) (*open completely*) The flowers slowly opened up in the warmth of the sun. (*b*) (*speak frankly*) The girl decided to open up and tell us everything. (*c*) (*emerge, develop*) New prospects have opened up for us this year. 2 (*a*) (*open completely*) He opened up the packing-cases and found that they were full of valuable old books. (*b*) (*make accessible, develop*) The pioneers opened up this land over a hundred years ago. The company has decided to open up this area for housing. (*c*) (*start*) They decided to open up a business in the town.
- **order + particle** (*order, with direction*) The general ordered up more men as reinforcements. They wanted us to go and so they ordered us out immediately. She ordered the little boy down from the high ladder. He doesn't like being ordered about by anyone.
- **own up** (*confess, admit, own*) He owned up to the crime. They hoped he would own up to having told the lie. Come on, own up!

P

- **pace + particle** (*walk with measured steps, with direction*) The worried man paced up and down.
- **pace out** (*measure by pates or strides*) They paced out the distance between the houses.
- **pack away** (*a*) (*store away*) She packed away the clothes until they would be needed again. (*b*) (*eat*) He can pack away more food than anyone else I know.
- **pack off** (*a*) (*send as a package or in a package*) He has packed the books off to his friend. (*b*) (*dismiss, send*) She always packs the children off to bed about seven.
- **pack up** 1 (*a*) (*do one's luggage*) I've been packing up, ready to go. (*b*) (*stop*) The men have packed up and gone home. (*c*) (*stop functioning*) = **pack in** (*d*) (*become transportable*) My books pack up easily.
- **pad + particle** (*move softly on pads or as if on pads, with direction*) The cat padded along. A lion was padding up and down inside the cage. He pads round in carpet slippers all day.
- **pad out** 1 (*fill out with extra material*) (*a*) The tailor padded out the shoulders of the coat. (*b*) The editor asked him to stop padding out his articles.
- **paint in** (*include or add by painting*) They painted in the sections which had been left empty.
- **paint on** 1 (*continue to paint*) He painted on through the night. 2 (*add on by painting*) They painted on the name of the ship.
- **paint out** (*remove or delete by using paint*) They painted out the names on the shop front.
- **paint up** (*improve by using paint*) They have painted the place up since I was last here.
- **pair off** 1 (*separate into pairs*) The young people soon paired off. 2 (*a*) (*divide or separate into pairs*)

The students have been paired off. He has been paired off with me. They paired us off for the purpose of the exercise. (*b*) (*couple for reproductive purposes*) They paired the animals off.

- **pal up** (*become friendly*) They have palled up again after the quarrel. I hope the two boys will pal up. He has palled up with some rather disreputable types.
- **palm off** (*pass by trickery*) He has palmed these shoddy goods off on to us. There should be a law against people palming off rubbish like this.
- **pan + particle** 1 (*move to present a panorama*) The camera panned out over the crowd. The TV cameraman panned up to bring in the aeroplanes. 2 Pan the camera over to include those people. Can you pan it down(wards) and then over to the left.
- **pan out** (*a*) (*turn out, develop*) Things didn't pan out well for them. Events may pan out better than expected.
- **paper over** (*a*) (*cover with paper*) They papered over the cracks in the wall. (*b*) (*attempt to conceal*) I think we must try to paper over this disagreement.
- **parcel out** (*share out in portions*) (*a*)) They parcelled out the food for the refugees. (*b*) The inheritance has not been kept together, but has been parcelled out among the family.
- **pass away** (*a*) (*die*) He passed away at midnight last night. (*b*) (*vanish, disappear*) The old cultural values have passed away.
- **pass down** 1 (*a*) (*hand down, transmit*) The tradition has been passed down from father to son. (*b*) (*send down through a hierarchy or organisation*) The story has been passed down that he bungled the negotiations.
- **pass for** (*be taken for, be recognized as*) She would pass for an American very easily. You surely don't think I

could pass for him, do you? She's 40, but I think she could pass for 25 without much trouble.
- **pass off** 1 (*go away*) I was feeling sick, but the feeling has passed off. 2 (*succeed in presenting*) She passed herself off as an American. They passed him off as a much younger man.
- **pass on** 1 (*a*) (*die*) He passed on in his sleep. (*b*) (*move on*) Let us pass on to a new subject. 2 (*a*) (*tell someone else*) Pass the news on that he is coming tomorrow.
- **pass out** (*a*) (*faint*) She passed out when she heard the bad news. He passed out from too much drinking. (*b*) (*graduate*) He has passed out with honours. *noun* **a passing-out parade**. (*c*) (*go on and away, move from*) He has passed out of our lives completely.
- **pass over** (*die*) He passed over in his sleep.
- **pass up** (*a*) (*forgo, waive*) He passed up the chance to go to France this summer. You should never pass up opportunities like these.
- **paste in** (*put in, insert or include by using paste*) He pasted the pictures in.
- **paste on** (*put on, by using paste*) He pasted the stickers on.
- **paste up** (*put up, by using paste*) He pasted the notice up.
- **pay up** 1 (*pay promptly*) I asked him to pay up. Pay up! 2 (*a*) (*settle promptly or fully*) Please pay up all you owe. He is a fully **paid-up** member of this club.
- **peak off** (*reach a maximum and fall off*) The numbers have begun to peak off. The sales peak off at this point.
- **peal out** (*ring out in peals, resound*) The bells pealed out.
- **peck out** (*remove or destroy by pecking*) The crows pecked out the eyes of the dead sheep.

- **pedal + particle** (*move by pedalling or using pedals, with direction*) The boy got on his bicycle and pedalled away. The girl was pedalling up and down in the street.
- **peel back** (*remove by stripping to one side*) He peeled back the plastic film.
- **peel off** 1 (*undress*) She peeled off and went to bed. 2 (*remove*) She peeled off her clothes and went to bed.
- **peep + particle** (*look quickly and often furtively, with direction*) He raised the edge of the curtain and we peeped through. He could see the children peeping in through the window.
- **peer + particle** (*look intently, with direction*) He was peering about in the dark, looking for something. The children peered out through the windows.
- **peg away** (*continue working*) He has been pegging away at that material for months.
- **peg down** (*hold or fix down with pegs*) They pegged the tent down securely.
- **peg out** 1 (*die, stop functioning*) The old man pegged out. This engine is going to peg out soon, if you don't do something. 2 (*mark out with pegs*) They pegged the area out.
- **pelt + particle** (*move very rapidly, with direction*) The car pelted along. I opened the door and the little boys pelted out.
- **pelt down** (*pour down violently*) The rain was pelting down (for all it was worth).
- **pension off** (*superannuate; dismiss from service with a pension*) Has he been pensioned off yet? I think they will pension him off soon. We do not want to be pensioned off and forgotten.
- **pent-up** (*suppressed, repressed*) He is full of pent-up resentments. They give you an impression of pent-up power.

- **pep up** 1 (*become cheerful*) She pepped up considerably when she heard the news. 2 (*make more cheerful, improve, fill with pep and energy*) He pepped me up a lot with his comments. He pepped the party up with his jokes. She asked him to pep her drink up with something stronger.
- **permit + particle** (*allow, with direction*) The doctor permits her up now for several hours a day, because of her steady improvement. Would you permit them in for a few minutes, to talk to you? The escort stood back from the door and permitted them through.
- **permit of** (*allow, intensive of* **permit**) This situation does not permit of an easy solution.
- **persuade + particle** (*move by persuading, with direction*) Do you think you could persuade them over to see me? She persuaded him up for a cup of coffee. They persuaded me in to shelter from the rain.
- **peter out** (*become exhausted, empty*) (*a*) The supply of coal has just petered out. The goldmine petered out years ago. (*b*) His ambitions slowly petered out in the face of opposition. Her enthusiasm for the project has completely petered out.
- **phase in** (*introduce in phases or stages*) They have decided to phase the new techniques in immediately. It will take years to phase in all these developments.
- **phase out** (*remove by phases or stages*) We really ought to phase these less successful products out. It will take a long time to phase out the obsolete laws.
- **pick at** (*a*) (*eat in tiny portions*) The birds picked at the bread crumbs. (*b*) (*eat listlessly*) He has just been picking at his food lately. (*c*) (*keep touching and scratching*) Stop picking at that scab. She picks at her face all the time. (*d*) (*adversely criticise in small ways*) He has been picking at your work for some time now.

- **pick away** (*remove or alter by small stages*) Some animal has picked away the side of the fence. If you pick away the covering, you can see the inscriptions underneath.
- **pick off** (*a*) (*collect or remove by picking*) They have picked off all the apples. (*b*) (*shoot individually*) The sniper picked off two of our sentries this morning. The marksman picked the enemy off one by one.
- **pick over** (*inspect, by lifting and feeling with the fingers*) She picked over the fruit. Customers were picking over the remnants left after the sale.
- **piece together** (*put together piece by piece*) (*a*) They pieced together the broken vase. The pottery dug up at that archaeological site needs to be carefully pieced together. (*b*) The detectives have slowly pieced together the whole astonishing story. I managed to piece together what had happened from what he told me.
- **pierce through** (*pierce, penetrate completely*) The arrow pierced him through.
- **pile off** (*jump off in a crowd*) The lorries stopped and the men piled off.
- **pile on** 1 (*jump on in a crowd*) The lorries drew up and the waiting soldiers piled on. 2 (*a*) (*put on in a heap*) He piled the stones on. (*b*) (*intensify*) They seem to enjoy piling on the bad news. (*c*) (*exaggerate*) Stop piling it on. She certainly piles it on.
- **pile up** 1 (*accumulate*) (*a*) The debris has piled up against that wall. (*b*) His debts have been piling up for quite some time. His work has piled up while he's been away. 2 (*accumulate*) (*a*) They had piled up a lot of earth in one corner of the garden. She piled up plenty of tinned food in case of an emergency. (*b*) He has piled up a lot of troubles for himself.

- **pilot + particle** (*guide, with direction*) The man piloted the ship in. Can find someone to pilot us out of here?
- **pine away** (*pine continuously*) She has been pining away since you left. That dog is pining away for its master.
- **pipe + particle** (*move by means of a pipe, with direction*) They piped the water away. The water was piped up from the valley. They decided to pipe the supply in from the next valley. The oil is piped out from this point.
- **pipe away** (*play a woodwind instrument continuously*). He has been piping away for the last two hours.
- **pipe down** (*be quiet*) I wish he would pipe down. Pipe down!
- **pipe in** (*bring in, accompanied by bagpipe music*) The haggis was piped in. The regimental band triumphantly piped the soldiers in.
- **pipe up** (*a*) (*speak up in a piping voice*) The child suddenly piped up that he wanted to go home. (*b*) (*speak up*) He piped up near the end of the meeting.
- **pitch + particle** (*a*) (*throw or compel, with direction*) He pitched the ball out (of the court). They pitched the materials in. (*b*) He was pitched out of that club. Pitch the paper over to me, please.
- **pitch in** (*participate*) I like the way he always pitches in and helps. Right, folks, pitch in!
- **pitch into** (*attack*) (*a*) The gang pitched into him and left him badly injured. (*b*) The opposition politicians pitched into his speech, criticising it point by point.
- **pitch out** (*a*) (*eject*) The car overturned and the driver was pitched out. (*c*) (*get rid of*) It's time you pitched those books out.
- **plan out** (*plan as fully as possible*) They planned out the trip (with care).

- **plane down** 1 (*descend in or like an aeroplane*) The glider planed down towards the meadow. 2 (*smooth down with a plane*) The carpenter planed the wood down.
- **plank down** (*put down, deposit briskly*) He planked the money down on the counter and asked for more beer.
- **plant out** (*lift and re-plant in the open*) These bulbs should now be planted out. When will you plant the flowers out in beds?
- **plaster down** (*stick, smooth down with plaster*) (*a*) He plastered the material down. (*b*) He plastered his hair down (with a new hair oil).
- **plaster on** (*put on thickly like plaster*) He plastered the butter on. He plastered on the hair oil.
- **play up to** (*flatter, ingratiate oneself with*) She is always playing up to people who may be able to help her.
- **plod + particle** (*walk slowly and heavily, with direction*) The oxen plodded on. The horse plodded back and forth.
- **plonk down** (*fall suddenly*) The apple plonked down on her lap.
- **plot out** (*a*) (*design fully or clearly*) They plotted out a plan of action. (*b*) (*mark out*) He plotted out the course which the ship should follow.
- **plough + particle** (*move as if ploughing, with direction*) The ship ploughed along through the heavy seas. The bulldozer was ploughing up and down.
- **plough in** (*mix in by ploughing*) They decided to plough the sand in. The builders ploughed in a lot of young trees when clearing this area for development.
- **plough up** (*a*) (*plough thoroughly*) This land should be ploughed up. The farmer ploughed up the whole area. (*b*) (*churn up*) The tanks have ploughed up a lot of mud.
- **pluck + particle** (*pull, gently or with small hand movements, with direction*) They plucked me aside from

the others. She plucked the hairs out. They plucked the surplus wool off. The gardener plucked all the weeds up.

- **pluck up** (*a*) (*find, develop*) The boy tried to pluck up enough courage to face the bully. I wish I could pluck up enough energy to do this work.
- **plug away** (*continue working*) He has been plugging away at that job for hours.
- **plug in** 1 (*attach with an electric plug*) Have you plugged in yet? 2 (*fix in with a plug*) Would you plug the light in? She wants to plug the radio in.
- **plug up** (*close or seal by means of plugs*) They have plugged up those holes under the wall.
- **plump for** (*choose*) I'll plump for bacon and eggs rather than breakfast cereal. He always plumps for the best that's going.
- **plump up** (*a*) (*fatten*) We have really plumped up these chickens. (*b*) (*fluff out, make appear fat*) She took the cushions and plumped them up a bit.
- **plunge + particle** (*plunge, rush, with direction*) The boys ran to the edge of the swimming pool and plunged in. The frightened horse plunged aside. Dolphins were plunging about in the bay.
- **plunge in** 1 (*take part eagerly*) They asked me to help, so I just plunged in. 2 (*thrust in violently or with some effort*) He plunged the dagger in to the hilt.
- **point + particle** (*indicate, run with a finger, with direction*) They pointed up to where the man was climbing. She pointed back to where the others were following. He pointed forward.
- **point out** (*a*) (*show*) Can you point him out to me, please? (*b*) (*mention*) I pointed out the difficulties. He pointed out that the work was nearly complete.

- **point up** (*emphasise*) His rudeness just points up her good manners.
- **poke about/around** (*make unwanted inquiries*) Those detectives have been poking about here again.
- **poke in** (*introduce, without welcome*) He has been poking in again, trying to find things out.
- **poke up** (*stir with a poker*) Can you poke up the fire?
- **polish off** (*finish completely*) He polished off the food.
- **polish up** (*a*) (*polish thoroughly*) They polished up the silverware till it shone. (*b*) (*improve*) I'll have to polish up my French before the holidays.
- **post up** (*put up for display*) He posted up the new regulations.
- **potter about/around** (*go about doing small jobs*) He is pottering about in the garden.
- **pounce out** (*leap out*) The cat pounced out on the bird.
- **pound + particle** (*move along quickly but heavily, with direction*) The herd of buffaloes pounded along. A horseman came pounding up with the news. The cavalry pounded down on the enemy.
- **pound down** (*pulverize, reduce by pounding*) They pounded down the stones to a fine powder.
- **pound up** (*reduce completely by pounding, pulverize thoroughly*) She pounded up the ingredients.
- **pour + particle** 1 (*flour, with direction*) The water poured out. The rain poured down. The troops poured past. Men and machines poured along the main highways. They opened the gates and supplies began to pour through. 2 She poured the water out. She poured the remains away. The general poured men in to replace the slaughtered battalions.
- **pour out** (*a*) She poured out her troubles. He poured his heart out to us. (*b*) She just poured out her feelings.

- **praise up** (*praise fully*) They have been praising you up to everyone they meet.
- **print out** (*a*) (*print and distribute*) They intend to print out thousands of these leaflets. (*b*) (*produce*) The computer has printed out the results you want. *noun* **a computer printout**.
- **prise out** (*extract by levering*) (*a*) He prised the nail out (of the door). (*b*) They intend to prise the information out of him somehow.
- **prise up** (*lift up by levering*) They want to prise up the flagstones and see what is underneath. He prised up the floorboards.
- **prod + particle** (*encourage to move by prodding or poking, with direction*) The oxen were prodded along. The sergeant prodded the men out of their beds. They opened the door and prodded the prisoner through.
- **promise away** (*give away by promising*) He has promised most of the money away to various people.
- **prop up** (*a*) (*support by means of props*) The men propped the old tunnel up with new timbers. (*b*) (*serve as a prop for*) The new timbers prop up the old mine tunnel. (*c*) (*support, maintain*) The regime has been propped up by several rich families.
- **propel + particle** (*direct, convey, with direction*) They propelled the men away. He propelled the car out.
- **prune away** (*cut away systematically*) (*a*) The gardener pruned away the ragged edges of the bush. (*b*) We must prune away some of our surplus staff.
- **pucker up** (*intensive of pucker*) The child's face puckered up and she began to cry.
- **puff + particle** (*move by means of light gusts of wind, with direction*) The breeze puffed the boats across from one side of the pond to the other. The wind puffed the scraps of paper in and out among the trees.

- **puff away** 1 (*a*) (*smoke continuously*) The old man puffed away at his pipe. He was pulling away on a big cigar. (*b*) (*move away with puffs of smoke*) The train puffed away. 2 (*expand*) He puffed out his chest and told us about his victory. She puffed out the story quite a lot.
- **puff up** (*swell*) Her face has puffed up after being stung by a bee. His eye looks very puffed up.
- **pull + particle** 1 (*move under power, with direction*) The train pulled along steadily. 2 (*impel by force, with direction*) He pulled the cork out of the bottle. She pulled the box up to where she wanted it. He pulled the materials over to his side of the table.
- **pull about** (*tug and shove*) They pulled him about rather violently.
- **pull away** (*a*) (*accelerate*) The car pulled away from the other vehicles. (*c*) (*pull steadily*) The sailors pulled away on the oars.
- **pull back** (a) (*hesitate, withdraw*) He pulled back from signing the document. (*b*) (*withdraw*) The general decided to pull his men back.
- **pull down** (*a*) (*demolish*) They pulled the old building down. (*b*) (*weaken*) This illness has pulled him down. (*c*) (*humiliate, criticise*) They intend to pull him down a peg or two.
- **pull off** (*complete successfully*) He pulled that deal off beautifully. They didn't manage to pull it off.
- **pull over** 1 (*a*) (*move aside*) The car pulled over to let the others past. 2 *noun* **a pullover** = a garment which is put on by pulling it over the head.
- **pull round** 1 (*get better after an illness or indisposition*) I expect he'll pull round. 2 (*make better, after an illness or indisposition*) This brandy will help pull you round.
- **pull through** 1 (*recover, from illness or trouble*) Oh, don't worry, you'll pull through. He was badly injured,

but he'll pull through. 2 (*help recover*) Somehow or other we'll pull him through, despite the injuries.
- **pull together** 1 (*co-operate*) I hope all the members of staff will pull together. 2 *Idiomatic reflexive = compose oneself*) I asked him to pull himself together. After breaking down and weeping, she tried hard to pull herself together. Pull yourself together.
- **pull up** 1 (*come to a halt, of a vehicle*) The car pulled up. 2 (*a*) (*stop*) He pulled the horses up. (*b*) (*check, reprimand*) The police pulled him up for speeding. The soldier was pulled up for having an untidy uniform.
- **pump + particle** (*transfer under pressure, with direction*) To get the oil to the tank on the roof they had to pump it up. The machine has been pumping away the water. The men tried to pump the liquid out. The firemen began pumping water in.
- **pump up** (*inflate*) He pumped up the bicycle tyre.
- **punch + particle** (*punch, with direction*) He punched the window in with his fist. They punched out little holes along the edge of the paper. The goalkeeper punched the ball aside. *noun* **a punch-up** (*a fight with the fists*) They had a punch-up over those girls. Don't start a punch-up here.
- **purse up** (*tighten, like the top of a purse*) She pursed up her lips.
- **push + particle** 1 (*move forcefully, with direction*) He pushed in through the crowd. They pushed on until darkness fell. They pushed upwards until they reached the top. 2 (*push, impel, with direction*) He pushed the barrow along. We tried to push the lid down, but couldn't. He pushed the hatch up. He opened the window and pushed himself out on to the ledge. She was in a hurry and pushed the others aside. He pushed the plate away.

- **push around/about** (*bully*) Stop pushing everybody about!
- **push for** (*demand*) The men are pushing for higher wages.
- **push on** 1 (*continue going*) Well, we'd better push on. The travellers pushed on without halting. 2 (*exhort, egg on*) They are pushing him on to take the exam.
- **push out** (*spout*) The plant is pushing out shoots.
- **push over** *Idiomatic noun* It's **a push-over** = it's very easy.
- **put in for** (*request*) They have put in for a change of doctor.
- **put off** (*a*) (*postpone*) They have put off the meeting because of the weather. (*b*) (*dismay, discourage*) Don't let his rough manner put you off. She has been put off by his offensive remarks.
- **put on** (*a*) (*don*) He put on his hat. (*b*) (*pretend*) You are just putting it on, aren't you? Stop putting it on! *noun* **a put-on**=a pretence.
- **put over** *Idiom*: put one over on someone= cheat him/her.
- **put through** (*a*) (*connect*) The operator will put you through now. Would you put me through to him now? (*b*) (*succeed in accomplishing*) They have put through some clever business deals in their time.
- **put up with** (*tolerate*) She puts up with a lot of insolence from those people. I wouldn't put up with his nonsense if I were you.
- **put upon** (*be coerced, forced, pass*) I will not be put upon!
- **puzzle out** (*puzzle or work out, to a solution*) They could not puzzle out his intentions. I wish I could puzzle out why he did it.

Q

- **queue up** (*form a queue*) The people began to queue up. We have been queuing up here for hours.
- **quicken up** 1 (*accelerate, increase*) The man's pace quickened up. 2 (*speed up, accelerate*) He quickened up his pace. The tempo of production has quickened up factory output.
- **quieten down** 1 (*become quiet, calm*) The noise of the wind has quietened down. He was very angry, but he has quietened down now. 2 (*make quiet*) I want you to quieten those children down.

R

- **rack up** (*score or log up*) He racked up a large number of points.
- **rail in** (*enclose with rails or a railing*) They railed the area in.
- **rail off** (*mark off or separate with rails or a railing*) They have railed off the enclosure.
- **raise up** (*Old, intensive of* **raise**) He has raised up a family of champions. He claimed he could raise up devils.
- **rake + particle** (*furrow or move with a rake, with direction*) The gardener raked the stones aside. The ground has been thoroughly raked over. They have raked the leaves out.
- **rake in** (*bring in quantities*) That gambling casino just rakes money in. He rakes in a lot of cash.
- **rake off** (*remove as a special profit or fee*) They rake off 10% for themselves. *noun* **a rake-off** = a special profit.

- **rake over** (*discuss, gossip about*) They like raking over old scandals.
- **rake up** (*unearth, discover*) They enjoy raking up new scandals. Where did you rake that story up?
- **ram + particle** (*push forcefully, with direction*) He rammed the bolt in. They rammed the logs through. He was rammed back against the wall by the rush of water. The government intends to ram this new legislation through.
- **ramble + particle** (*walk for enjoyment in the countryside, with direction*) They just rambled along. A group of people rambled up. They rambled on through the woods.
- **ramble on** (*talk on without stopping, in a rather aimless way*) He rambled on about his unfulfilled ambitions. I wish she wouldn't ramble on and on about her children.
- **rampage about/around** (*go about in a dangerous, uncontrolled manner*) Gangs of teenagers were rampaging about, breaking things. Looting soldiers rampaged about in the town centre.
- **rap out** (*a*) (*signal by rapping or knocking*) He rapped out a morse message. Something was rapping out sounds on the table. (*b*) (*state clearly and briskly*) He rapped out a command.
- **read back** (*repeat a reading of; read in return*) He read back the list of names to me, and I checked them off one by one. Please read it back to me.
- **read in** (*add in by inference*) You shouldn't try to read in (to this matter) things which aren't there. Don't read things in to what I say.
- **read on** (*a*) (*continue to read*) He read on through the afternoon. (*b*) (*read further*) When you have done the exercise, read on to page 45. Now read on.

- **read out** (*read aloud*) He read the proclamation out. The pupils took turns in reading out their work.
- **read over** (*read fully*) The editor read over the manuscript. I'd like you to read this over for me.
- **read up** (*learn up by reading, study*) He has been reading the subject up. I believe he has started reading up anthropology.
- **reckon on** (*base one's assumptions on*) You should reckon on having to deal with more than one problem. Does he seriously reckon on winning? She didn't reckon on six extra dinner guests.
- **reckon up** (*assess, count up*) He has begun reckoning up the odds against success. Have you reckoned up the casualties of this attack?
- **reckon with** (*expect to encounter*) I didn't reckon with this kind of opposition. You shall have to reckon with her obstinacy.
- **reckon without** (*expect not to have*) You must reckon without our help in this matter. He reckoned without their interference.
- **reel in** (*draw in fishing law on its reel*) The man reeled in and went home without catching anything. 2 (*draw in on a fishing lust with its reel*) He reeled in a beautiful trout.
- **reel off** (*state quickly, accurately and at length*) He reeled off the names of all the people concerned in the affair. She can reel off great chunks of Shakespeare.
- **reel out** (*release or unbind on a reel*) The angler reeled out his fishing line. I reeled out more thread.
- **reel up** (*draw in on a reel*) They reeled up the line and stored it away.
- **rein back** 1 (*restrain a horse or harnessed animal*) The rider reined back. 2 (*a*) (*restrain by pulling on reins*) The rider reined his horse back. (*b*) (*restrain*) You should rein back your passions.

- **rein up** 1 (*stop a horse or harnessed animal*) The rider reined up. 2 (*stop by pulling on reins*) He reined up his horse.
- **remain in** (*stay indoors*) We remained in because of the heavy rain.
- **remain out** (*stay outside*) The children remained out because of the good weather.
- **remain up** (*stay up after bedtime*) The children remained up because their uncle had come to see them.
- **render down** (*reduce to an oil*) The fatty substances have been rendered down.
- **render up** (*surrender, give*) The captain has rendered up his castle to the enemy.
- **report back** 1 (*bring back a report*) Our correspondent has just reported back from the front line. I expect them to report back here as soon as they arrive. 2 (*send back in report form*) She reported the story back as soon as she could.
- **rest up** (*have a complete rest*) She is resting up for a few weeks.
- **rev up** (*increase the revs or revolutions in*) The mechanic revved up the engine. He loves revving that sports car up.
- **ride + particle** 1 (*ride, with direction*) They rode along. The horsemen rode up to the gate. She rode away. 2 He rode the horse back to the stable. They rode the animals away. She rode her cycle back to town.
- **ride down** (*attack and knock, down while riding*) The enemy cavalry rode our men down.
- **ride out** (*a*)(*survive by riding at anchor*) The ship rode out the storm. We can ride out the hurricane by staying here. (*b*) (*survive through patience or endurance*) She can ride this business out. The company has managed to ride out this trade depression.

- **ride up** (*rise steadily up*) I don't like this skirt because it keeps riding up.
- **rig out** (*clothe*) She rigged the children out in new dresses. He has been rigged out in a new uniform. *noun* **a-rig-out** = a set of clothes, a uniform.
- **rig up** (*a*) (*fit up the rigging or rope work of*) They rigged the ship up efficiently. (*b*) (*fit up*) He can rig up all sorts of useful gadgets if you ask him. The terrorists rigged up a booby-trap for the security forces. (*c*) (*contrive*) Is this one of the schemes you like rigging up? I'm sure he has rigged something up for us.
- **ring back** 1 (*call back on the telephone*) I'll ring back in ten minutes. 2 (*a*) (*re-contact, by telephone*) I'll 'ring you back in ten minutes. (*b*) (*open with a flourish*) They have rung back the curtains on a new show.
- **ring in** (*introduce by ringing bells*) The Scots like to ring in the New Year.
- **ring off** (*close a telephone conversation*) I'd better ring off now.
- **rinse out** 1 (*come out through rinsing with water*) These colours won't rinse out. 2 (*clean out by rinsing*) She rinsed out the cups. He rinsed out his mouth. You must rinse the shampoo out of your hair.
- **rip + particle** (*move quickly, with direction*) The motorbikes ripped along. He likes ripping up and down on his bicycle. The sports car ripped away in a trail of exhaust.
- **rip out** (*tear out with an effort*) She ripped out the pockets of the coat.
- **rip up** (*tear up with an effort*) He ripped up the documents. They ripped up the floorboards.
- **rise up** (*intensive of rise*) The hills rise up to six thousand feet. A strange creature rose up out of the mud. Smoke

rose up from the crater of the volcano. The people may rise up and destroy the tyrant.
- **roam + particle** (*wander, with direction*) The herds of buffalo roam about freely. The tribes roamed up from the plains to the mountains. I would love to roam away into those wonderful forests.
- **roar + particle** (*move with a roaring noise, with direction*) The huge machines roared off. Cars were roaring away from the starting-point. A jet plane roared in.
- **roar out** 1 (*give out a roar*) The lion roared out. 2 (*give out with a roar, or in a roaring voice*) The lion roared out its frustration. The champion roared out a challenge.
- **roof in** (*cover over with a roof*) The area has now been roofed in.
- **root for** (*cheer*) I always root for my favorite team. I'll be rooting for you on the great day.
- **root out** (*a*) (*remove by the roots*) He rooted out the weeds. (*b*) (*extirpate*) We must root out this evil. It is necessary to root out corruption in government.
- **root up** (*pull up by the roots*) Pigs love rooting things up with their noses.
- **rope off** (*mark off or separate with ropes*) This area has been roped off for the judges to use.
- **rope together** (*bring or tie together with ropes*) The animals have been roped together.
- **rot away** 1 (*rot, decay slowly and completely*) The dead body was rotting away. The wood had rotted away. 2 (*cause to rot completely*) The damp rots everything away eventually.
- **rot off** (*come off through rotting, decay*) The surface has rotted off.
- **rough in** (*fill in roughly*) He roughed in the rest of the sketch with a piece of charcoal.

- **rough out** (*sketch out roughly*) He roughed out the design, just to give us an idea of what he intended.
- **rough up** (*a*) (*make rough*) He roughed up her hair. (*b*) (*assault, but not too violently*) The gang decided to rough him up, as a warning to others. He has been roughed up a bit.
- **roughen up** (*make rough, objects*) The surface has to be roughened up before you put the tiles on.
- **round down** (*bring down to the lower whole figure*) The prices of the goods have all been rounded down.
- **round off** (*finish off welt*) The debate was rounded off by the chairman. They have rounded off their work and will write a detailed report.
- **round out** (*finish very fully*) He intends to round out his work before presenting his final analysis. This is good stuff, but it needs to be rounded out.
- **round (up)on** (*attack, turn violently on*) (*a*) (*lit*) The desperate animal rounded upon its attackers. (*b*) He rounded upon his tormentors with furious countercharges. She rounded on her critics.
- **rout out** (*get out of bed*) They routed the poor fellow out at six a.m.
- **row + particle** 1 (*row, with direction*) He rowed along steadily. The oarsmen rowed up to the jetty. I watched the fishermen row in. 2 He rowed the boat along steadily. The oarsmen rowed the boat up to the jetty. They rowed their boat in.
- **rub away** 1 (*rub continuously*) He rubbed away for hours to clean that old brass plate. 2 (*erode by rubbing*) Countless washerwomen have rubbed the stones away. The name on the brass plate has been rubbed away.
- **rub down** (*a*) (*clean or dry down by rubbing*) She rubbed the horse down. *n* **a rubdown**. (*b*) (*smooth down*) He rubbed the wood down with sandpaper.

- **rummage about/around** (*search untidily about*) She rummaged about in the drawer for a pencil. I like rummaging around in old shops.
- **rummage out** (*get out by rummaging*) They rummaged out some old clothes for the jumble sale.
- **run + particle** (*run, with direction*) The children were running about happily. He ran away in fear. She ran up and hugged me. The boys ran out to play.
- **run about/around** (*convey about, in a car*) I'll be glad to run you about while you're in town.
- **run after** (*a*) (*pursue*) They have been running after him all day. He has been running after her for months, but she isn't interested in him at all. She runs after everything in trousers. (*b*) (*serve, care for urn in a servile way*) She runs after her children all the time. I'm not going to spend my life running after you!
- **run at** (*attack, throw oneself upon*) He ran at them, sword in hand.
- **run along** 1 (*go away*) Run along! Run along now, children! 2 (*convey along, in a car*) I'll run you along to the station in a few minutes.
- **run back** (*a*) (*flow back*) The water began to run back into the depression as fast as they pumped it out. (*b*) (*take back, in a car*) I'll run you back home after the show. (*c*) (*re-wind*) She ran the tape back after hearing it. The projectionist runs the film back at the end of every performance.
- **run in** 1 (*flow in*) Rivulets of water were running in everywhere. 2 (*a*) (*convey in, a car*) I'll run you in to the station in a few minutes. (*b*) (*bring slowly into full use*) He is running in his new car. New cars sometimes have a notice on them 'Running in, please pass'. (*c*) (*arrest*)

The police have run him in again. (*d*) (*introduce*) They ran the liquid in through a tube.
- **run into** (*a*) (*meet by chance*) I ran into some old friends I hadn't seen for years. (*b*) (*collide with*) The car ran into a lamp standard. He ran into the back of a bus. (*c*) (*encounter*) You may run into some difficulties in that country. He has run into trouble in his job. (*d*) (*accumulate*) He has run into debt. (*e*) (*add up to*) His total income runs into six figures. Her book has run into four editions already.
- **run out of** (*begin to lose, lose*) We are running out of water. He ran out of hope long ago. I have run out of money. *Idiom*: to run Out of time=to have no time left.
- **run over** 1 (*a*) (*flow over*) The water rose rapidly and began to run over. The bath is running over! (*b*) (*visit briefly*) She ran over to her neighbor's to borrow some milk. I'll run over and see him tomorrow. 2 (*a*) (*recapitulate*) Let's just run over the story again. I'll run over your part with you. They ran over what happened to refresh their memories. (*b*) (*re-read*) She quickly ran over her notes. 3 (*a*) (*knock dawn, with a car*) The bus ran him over. He was run over by a bus. (*b*) (*play fully*) He ran the tape over and listened carefully. I'll run it over once again.
- **run through** 1 (*flow through*) The water runs through by means of this conduit. 2 (*a*) (*use up, consume*) He ran through the family fortune in a year. (*b*) (*read briefly*) He ran through the text a few minutes before he was due to speak. (*c*) (*rehearse*) Let's just run through the thing one more time. They ran through it again to get it right. *noun* **a run through** = a brief rehearsal. (*d*) (*recapitulate*) I would like just to run through the important points again,

if I may. 3 (*a*) (*transfix violently*) He ran his opponent through with a sword.
- **run up against** (*encounter*) He ran up against trouble in his new job. I ran up against some old acquaintances last week.
- **rust in** (*become fixed in through rust*) There is a risk that these screws will rust in.
- **rust up** 1 (*become rusty*) The car has rusted up badly. 2 (*make rusty*) This damp climate rusts cars up in no time at all. The equipment is all rusted up.
- **rustle up** (*provide, obtain, get hold of*) Can you rustle up some men to help us? She said she would rustle up some coffee.

S

- **saddle up** 1 (*put a saddle on a horse, preparatory to riding*) The men saddled up. 2 (*put a saddle on*) They saddled up their horses.
- **sag down** (*intensive of* **sag**) The canvas was sagging down under the weight of water.
- **sally forth** (*sally out, come out eagerly or vigorously*) The defenders sallied forth to meet the foe. I sallied forth one fine morning to seek adventure.
- **sally out** (*come out in a rush, come out confidently*) The defenders sallied out to attack the enemy.
- **salt away** (*a*) (*put away, preserved in salt*) He salted the meat away. (*b*) (*store away, save, hoard*) She has salted away her money somewhere. The tycoon has salted his profits away in Switzerland.
- **salt down** (*preserve with salt*) He salted down the meat and stored it away.

- **sandpaper down** (*rub down or smooth down with sandpaper*) The carpenter sandpapered down the surface.
- **scoop out** (*get out with a scoop or a scooping movement*) He scooped the dirt out with his hand. She scooped the raisins out (of the tin).
- **scoop up** (*pick up with a scoop or a scooping movement*) She scooped the raisins up from the floor. He scooped up his small son and carried him away. The machine scoops up the earth and dumps it over there.
- **scoot + particle** (*move swiftly, with direction*) Just scoot along and tell them I'm coming. The fish were scooting in and out of the weeds. Several little boats were scooting past.
- **scorch + particle** (*move very rapidly as if scorching the road, with direction*) The car just scorched along. The racing cars scorched off from the starting line. He scorched away on his motorbike.
- **score off** 1 (*delete by drawing a line*) He scored their names off and wrote in some others. 2 (*gain a victory against*) She likes to score off people when she can.
- **score out** (*delete completely, by drawing a line*) He scored out the names. She scored out her mistakes.
- **score up** (*mark up as part of a score*) They have scored up quite a lot of runs. The games were scored up on the board.
- **scour about/around** (*search diligently about*) She has been scouring about all over town for a certain kind of sausage.
- **scour out** (*a*) (*clean out by scouring*) She scoured out the pots. (*b*) The general hopes to scour the enemy out.
- **scout about/around** (*move about like a scout, or for purposes of scouting*) They scouted about for a good

place to camp. Scout about for something you like, get it, and send the bill to me.
- **scout out** (*a*) (*investigate fully*) They scouted out the terrain ahead of the army. (*b*) (*hunt out, find, discover*) He has scouted out some excellent wines. Trust you to scout out the best bargains.
- **scramble + particle** (*scramble, move quickly on hands and feet, with direction*) They scrambled down from the top of the cliff. He scrambled up to the ledge. I watched them scramble along to where the injured man was lying.
- **scramble up** (*mix up completely*) The materials were all scrambled up. The letters of the alphabet were scrambled up as part of the game.
- **scratch away** (*a*) (*scratch continuously*) He scratched away at his pimples all the time. The chickens were scratching away at the bare earth. (*b*) (remove by scratching) He scratched away the surface with a knife, and found gold underneath.
- **scratch up** (*a*) (*dig up by scratching*) The birds scratch up some worms from time to time. (*b*) (*find*) I'll manage to scratch some money up somehow. He scratched up a team from various sources.
- **scream out** (*a*) (*emit a scream, shriek*) She screamed out in terror. (*b*) (*email as a scream*) She screamed out a warning.
- **screen off** (*partition with a screen*) The working area is screened off completely. The patient in the corner bed was screened off from the other patients (in the hospital ward).
- **screw down** (*fix down with screws or by screwing*) They screwed the planks down and covered them with asbestos.

- **screw on** (*fix on with screws or by screwing*) They screwed the planks on firmly.
- **screw in** (*fix in as a screw or by screwing*) The joiner screwed the nails in. They screwed the light brackets in.
- **screw off** (*remove by taking out the screws or unscrewing*) The joiner screwed the lamp brackets off and took them away.
- **scribble away** 1 (*a*) (*scribble, make meaningless marks continuously*) The little girl loves scribbling away on pieces of paper. (*b*) (*write continuously but badly*) He scribbles away year in year out, but no one will publish his stuff. 2 (*spend in writing*) He scribbles his time away when he could be doing something useful.
- **scribble down** (*write down in a scribble*) He scribbled down some names and telephone numbers.
- **scribble out** (*write out in a scribble*) He scribbled out a note and left it on the table.
- **scrub away** 1 (*scrub continuously*) She scrubbed away at the doorstep until it was spotless. 2 (*remove by scrubbing*) I tried to scrub the stains away.
- **scrub down** (*clean down by scrubbing or rubbing hard*) They scrubbed the walls down. He scrubbed himself down.
- **scrub off** (*clean off by scrubbing*) They scrubbed the dirty marks off. I'll have to scrub off all the muck.
- **scrub out** (*remove or delete fully by scrubbing*) He scrubbed the marks out with a wet cloth and a brush.
- **scrub up** (*wash thoroughly, before treating a patient or performing an operation*) While the surgeon was scrubbing up, the anesthetist gave the patient an injection.
- **scud + particle** (*move swiftly, with direction*) The little ship scudded in from the open sea. Clouds were scudding

along in great streamers. Small boats were scudding back and forward.
- **scurry + particle** (*move hastily or quickly, With direction*) The small animals scurried along. The little girl scurried up breathlessly. The boy scurried away to find his friends.
- **seal in** (*enclose or close in by sealing*) Some prisoners were deliberately sealed in and abandoned. The remains of the king were sealed in (to the, tomb).
- **seal up** (*a*) (*close up fully, by sealing*) The doors were officially sealed up. The entrance to the tomb was sealed up. (*b*) The whole matter is now sealed up and finished. He hopes to seal things up soon.
- **search about/around** (*look around, search in an area*) The men were searching. about for something in the bushes. The police had been searching around all day, stopping people and asking questions.
- **search after/for** (*seek*) He is searching after something unattainable. She is searching for the truth.
- **see to** (*a*) (*undertake, attend to*) He sees to the various needs of the community. I'll see to it that you are: not inconvenienced. (Please) see to it (immediately). (*b*) (*mend, fix, repair*) These shoes need seeing to. Your cough ought to be seen to before it. gets any worse.
- **see up** 1 (*look upwards*) We could see up into the loft from the bottom of the stairs. 2 (*escort or conduct up*) He saw us up to the main office.
- **seek after** (*intensive of seek*) She is seeking after a better life.
- **seek out** (*go to find, look hard for*) I sought him out in the older part of the town. He seeks out all the new arrivals at the hotel and offers his services as a guide.
- **seep away** (*escape through seepage, drain slowly away*) The water took a week to seep away.

- **seep in** (*get in through seepage, drain slowly in*) Water has begun to seep in through these boards.
- **seep out** (*get out through seepage, drain slowly out*) The liquid is seeping out (of its container) into the ground.
- **seize up** (*lock hard into position*) The engine has seized up. His back seized up when he bent down.
- **seize (up)on** (*grasp hold of; intensive of seize*) He seized upon my offer in desperation. They will seize upon any help they are given. He will seize upon any excuse not to go.
- **sell off** (*liquidate*) He has sold off his business. Everything has been sold off to pay his debts.
- **sell up** 1 (*sell one's major assets*) They have sold up and gone. I'll just have to sell up now, to get some ready cash. 2 (*a*) (*force to sell*) His creditors have sold him up. (*b*) (*intensive of sell*) They sold up the property.
- **send + particle** (*send, with direction*) When he arrived I sent him in. If you talk any more I shall have to send you out. He sent his sister up to see their mother who was in bed. They sent the boy back with their reply.
- **send after** (*send someone to search for*) I've sent after him and hope he'll get the message.
- **send along** (*intensive of send*) Would you send them along to see me when they come. Just send him along, please.
- **send away** (*a*) (*dispatch*) They sent the goods away immediately. (*b*) (*banish, send elsewhere*) I sent him away because I was tired of his idle chatter.
- **send for** (*summon, order*) They sent for the doctor. The boss has sent for me. He sent for a pint of beer.
- **send in** (*submit or dispatch to an authority*) He has sent in his report. The correspondent sent in his dispatches regularly. He sent in his application immediately.

- **send in for** (*request, as from exterior to interior*) The painters sent in for more paint.
- **send off** (*see off, accompany or attend while departing*) There was a large crowd to send him off. *noun* **a send-off**. *Example:* The send-off was heart-warming.
- **send out** (*a*) (*dispatch*) They sent him out to get the newspaper. (*b*) (*circulate*) The company is sending out leaflets to all its contacts. (*c*) (*emit, give out*) This lamp sends out a powerful beam. This fire sends out a lot of heat. **send forth**. Some stars send out vast quantities of radiation. That radio transmitter sends signals out constantly.
- **send out for** (*request, as from interior to exterior*) The workmen in the building sent out for some sandwiches.
- **send up** (*a*) (*cause to go up*) They have sent up several space ships this year. The climbers sent two men up to investigate the rockfall. The distressed ship sent up a flare. (*b*) (*satirize*) The students here love to send up the staff. *noun* **a send-up** = a satire or mocking representation. (*c*) (*blow up, explode*) The terrorists sent the bridge up.
- **send up for** (*request, as from below to above*) The men in the hole sent up for more equipment.
- **separate out** (*intensive of separate*) They separated out. the various elements in the problem.
- **serve out** (*a*) (*distribute while serving*) The waiters served out the second course. She served out very ample helpings to her guests. (*b*) (*serve to the end*) The prisoners must serve out their time (in jail).
- **serve up** (*a*) (*serve or bring to the table*) She served up the food piping hot. I don't like serving things up cold. Are you ready to serve up? (*b*) (*provide, deliver*) He serves up some powerful propaganda.
- **set about** (*a*) (*begin, start*) He set about the work systematically. She set about writing the essay. I don't

know how to set about it. How do you set about a thing like that? (b) (*attack*) The gang set about him and injured him badly. They set about each other furiously.
- **set apart** (a) (*place separately*) These objects should be set apart from the others. (b) (*differentiate*) These qualities set him apart from the rest of the group.
- **set (up)on** (*attack*) The thieves set upon him and beat him senseless.
- **settle in** (*install oneself*) The new family have settled in. I hope you are all settling in satisfactorily.
- **settle up** 1 (*bring a matter to a conclusion*) It's time we settled up. I'll settle up with them soon. 2 (*intensive of settle, pay*) He settled up the outstanding bills. Let's settle the bill up together.
- **settle (up)on** (*decide on*) They have settled upon a house near the river. I don't know what dress she finally settled on.
- **sew on** (*sew into position*) She sewed the buttons on.
- **sew up** (a) (*sew as completely as possible, close by sewing*) She sewed the tear up. The seams have been sewn up. The surgeon sewed up the wound. The materials were sewn up in a sack. (b) (*finalize satisfactorily, organise efficiently*) He has the whole matter sewn up. It's all sewn up.
- **shade in** 1 (a) (*blend in or harmonise in easy stages*) The lights shade in beautifully. (b) (*fill in with pencil, charcoal etc*) When he finished the outlines, he started shading in. 2 (a) (*bring in by stages*) The technicians shaded the light in. (b) I imagine you can shade your activities in gradually, without anyone noticing. (c) (*fill in with pencil or charcoal, etc.*) When he finished the outlines, he started to shade in the rest.
- **shade off** (*move by stages, in a continuum*) The reds slowly shade off into pink.

- **shake down** 1 (*sleep*) Let's shake down here. 2 (*cause to fall by shaking*) He tried to shake the apples down from the tree.
- **shake out** (*a*) (*get out by shaking*) He shook the sweets out (of the bag). She shook the insects out. (*b*) (*loosen or straighten by shaking*) He shook out the empty sack. They shook out canvas. The sails were shaken out.
- **shamble + particle** (*shamble, walk heavily, slowly, with direction*) The great hairy creature shambled along. The tired prisoners shambled in to their cells. Tired and wounded soldiers were shambling past in the gathering darkness.
- **share out** (*share evenly, distribute, divide out*) They shared Out the food carefully. The money has been shared out. *noun* **a share-out.**
- **sharpen up** 1 (*become sharp or sharper*) The wind is sharpening up. 2 (*a*) (*make sharp or sharper*) The men sharpened up their knives. (*b*) This tension certainly sharpens up one's senses. You need to sharpen up your wits!
- **shave off** (*remove by shaving or planning*) He shaved off his beard. I think you should shave off your moustache. The carpenter shaved some wood off (with a plane).
- **shear off** 1 (*come off completely, break off, become suddenly detached*) The wheel sheared off and fell to the ground. 2 (*a*) (*cut off with shears*) He sheared the wool off. (*b*) (*cut off, remove by cutting*) They sheared off the ragged edges.
- **shepherd + particle** (*guide like a shepherd, lead, ushers with direction*) He shepherded us in. She shepherded her guests out. The warden shepherded everyone over to the window.
- **shift + particle** 1 (*move house, with direction*) They have shifted away from this area. When the tenants left

he shifted down to the flat below. 2 (*shift, transfer, with direction*) He shifted the luggage up to his flat. I think I'll shift this cupboard down to the living-room. He has shifted the rug away from the window.
- **shift away** (*transfer one's attention or interest*) He has shifted away from this policy.
- **shin down** (*climb down*) The boys shinned down from the roof.
- **shin up** (*climb up*) He shinned up onto the roof.
- **shine away** 1 (*shine continuously*) The lamp in the window shone away for hours. 2 (*shine to one side*) Please shine that light away (from my eyes).
- **shine down** 1 (*shine from above*) The sun shone down. 2 (*cause to shine from above*) Shine the torch down here, please.
- **shine in** 1 (*shine from outside*) The light shone in. 2 (*cause to shine from outside*) Shine the torch in, please.
- **shine on** 1 (*a*) (*continue to shine*) The stars shone on into a pale morning. The sun shone on for hours in a cloudless sky. (*b*) (*shine on to a position*) The light shines on from over there and illuminates the stage. 2 (*cause to shine on to a position*) Shine the torch on so that we can read the labels.
- **shine out** 1 (*a*) (*shine from inside*) The rays of a lamp shone out through the window. (*b*) (*shine suddenly*) A light shone out in the dark wall of the house. 2 (*cause to shine from inside*) Shine the torch out, please.
- **shine up** 1 (*shine from below*) The light shone up. 2 (*a*) (*cause to shine from below*) Shine the torch up into the rafters, please. (*b*) (*shine or polish as much as possible*) He shone his shoes up till they gleamed. I think I'll go and shine up the car a bit.
- **shove + particle** (*push, with direction*) The postman shoved the letters in. The boy shoved the toys out. She

shoved the food away, untouched. They shoved the boxes along, one by one.

- **shove off** (*leave, casually*) Well, we'd better be shoving off. He shoved off about an hour ago. Oh, shove off!
- **shove over** (*move over, to make room*) Shove over, I want to sit down.
- **shovel + particle** (*move with a shovel or spade, with direction*) He shovelled the earth away. They shovelled more soil in till the hole was filled. The workmen shovelled the stuff out.
- **show + particle** (*show, conduct, with direction*) The usher showed us in to our seats. The guards showed the visitors out. We were shown up to the new office. They were taken to the house and shown over/round.
- **show up** 1 (*appear, turn up*) He showed up when we least expected him. She'll show up when it suits her. They showed up again in Brazil a year later. I didn't expect you to show up here. 2 (*humiliate, shame*) She likes to show people up in public. Don't show us up by wearing something absurd. He showed his parents up rather badly.
- **shrivel up** (*a*) (*curl and dry up, to die*) The leaves are shrivelling up because of the terrific heat. The plant just shrivelled up. It turned yellow and shrivelled up. (*b*) I just shrivelled up when he looked at me. Do you expect me to shrivel up just because you criticize me?
- **shrug off** (*reject or dismiss with a shrug*) He shrugged off their complaints. She just shrugged the whole matter off. Please don't just shrug this off!
- **shuffle + particle** (*shuffle, move without raising feet, with direction*) The old man shuffled in. The prisoners shuffled dejectedly past. Several miserable refugees shuffled over, looking for food.

- **shuffle off** (*a*) (*discard, get rid of*) The snake shuffles off its skin once a year. (*b*) He shuffled off his old friends when he became famous.
- **shunt + particle** 1 (*divert, with direction*) A train shunted past. The engines shunted in and halted. 2 (*a*) The men shunted the engines in. He shunted the train out from the sidings. (*b*) Can you shunt those papers over, please? He shunted the stuff across to us for examination.
- **shuttle + particle** (*move to and fro, with direction*) The train shuttled back and forward. The goods wagons shuttled in and out. Papers keep shuttling around in this place.
- **shut away** (*lock away, isolate*) The animals are shut away in that hut all day long. They feel very shut away in that remote little cottage. He is afraid that the doctor will shut him away in a mental hospital.
- **shut down** 1 (*close completely*) The shop has shut down because of lack of trade. 2 (*a*) They have shut the shop down. The factory has been shut down (from lack of orders). *noun* **a shutdown** = a closure, a complete stoppage. (b) She shut the lid down.
- **shut in** (*seal or lock in, enclose*) She feels rather shut in this house. If you close that door you can shut the noise in.
- **shut off** (*a*) (*stop, shut completely, prevent from functioning*) would you shut the electricity off, please? The current has been shut off. They have shut off the water supply. (*b*) (*separate, isolate*) They feel shut off from all human contact on this island. We are really shut off here.
- **shy away** (*a*) (*react against something through fear, aversion or shyness*) The horse shied away. Don't shy away, please. (*b*) (*avoid*) He shies away from problems.

- **sift out** (*a*) (*separate out by using a sieve; isolate by using a sieve*) The farmers sifted out the good seed. He sifted out the wheat from the chaff. (*b*) The detectives tried to sift out the useful information from the irrelevant.
- **sign away** (*lose by signing, without sufficient thought*) You have just signed away a fortune. He signed away all his rights to the invention.
- **sign in** 1 (*indicate one's arrival by signing a register*) They signed in last night around eleven o'clock. 2 (*help gain admittance by signing*) He signed us in to his club. Can you find someone to sign me in?
- **simmer down** (*a*) (*become slowly cooler, after boiling*) The water has simmered down a bit, and you can use it. (*b*) His temper has simmered down and you may be able to reason with him. Come on, simmer down!
- **sing away** (*sing continuously*) She sings away for hours. The birds were singing away in the trees. 2 (*remove, or dismiss by singing*) Sing all your troubles away.
- **sing on** (*continue to sing*) They sang on for hours after the main party broke up.
- **sing out** (*a*) (*sing loudly*) The choirmaster urged them to sing out (for all they were worth) (*b*) (*shout out, perhaps melodiously*) She sang out when she heard the good news 2 (*a*) The choir sang the words out with great vigour. (*b*) He sang out something about getting promotion.
- **sing up** (*sing more loudly*) Sing up, sopranos, I can't hear you!
- **single out** (*distinguish or pick out for special treatment*) We singled him out as one of the most talented students. You have been singled out from all the others for this job. I don't know why they keep singling me out for abuse. He seems to have been singled out for all the nasty jobs.
- **sink down** (*a*) (*intensive of sink*) The sun slowly sank down in the west. She sank down on her knees. (*b*) (*go

down as fully as possible) He sank down out of sight when the enemy patrol came past.
- **sip up** (*sip as fully as possible or until all gone*) The little girl sipped up the lemonade.
- **siphon off** (*a*) (*remove or transfer by means of a siphon*) Someone has siphoned off my petrol! (*b*) The department is good at siphoning off funds from one area to another. They have siphoned the money off for their own use.
- **sit about/around** (*sit doing nothing in particular*) He just sits about all day. I wish I could just sit about and dream.
- **sit back** (*a*) (*sit well back, lean back while sitting*) He sat back in his chair and looked at me. Sit back and listen to this. (*b*) (*keep out of the way, become a spectator*) Do you expect me to sit back and do nothing.? They won't sit back and let you do it.
- **sit down** (*take a seat*) He sat down in the most comfortable chair. Ask them to sit down.
- **sit in** (*a*) (*sit in a place, for a special purpose*) She sits in for me sometimes, when I go shopping. He sits in with the patients while the nurse has a rest. (*b*) (*replace*) I shall sit in for you while you go to the shops. He's sitting in for his friend today. (*c*) (*demonstrate by sitting in a place*) Some of the students are sitting in at the Faculty Office. *noun* **a sit-in** = a passive seated demonstration.
- **sit in on** (*attend, as a visitor*) I'd like you to sit in on this meeting. She sat in on the whole debate.
- **sit out** 1 (*sit outside in the open air*) They sat out until the sun went in. 2 (*a*) (*attend by sitting, until completely finished*) I somehow managed to sit the meeting out. They sat out the play. (*b*) (*Dancing: not take part in*) I'll sit this dance out. May I sit this one out?
- **skim + particle** (*skim or move lightly, over a surface, with direction*) The hydrofoil skimmed along. Little

boats were skimming back and forward, across the lake. The water birds skimmed across.
- **skim off** (*a*) (*remove from the surface*) She skimmed the cream off the milk. (*b*) He always skims off the best students for his classes.
- **skim through** (*read quickly through, read superficially*) I don't have time to do more than skim through the book. He skimmed through. the essay (quickly).
- **skip + particle** (*hop, with direction*) She skipped up and down. The others were skipping about excitedly. She skipped past on her way to school.
- **skip across** (*visit quickly, and perhaps briefly*) He skipped across to Spain.
- **skip off** (*decamp, abscond, make off*) The accountant skipped off with the money.
- **skip over** (*pass over, omit, ignore*) I'll skip over your rudeness. Let's skip over these points and come to the main argument.
- **skirt round** (*a*) (*try to avoid, circumvent*) They skirted round the town and made for the hills. (*b*) They usually prefer to skirt round problems rather than face them squarely.
- **skive off** (*go away, to avoid work*) He has skived off somewhere. Trust him to skive off when we need him.
- **skulk + particle** (*walk in a stealthly way, with direction*) These men have been skulking about again. He skulked in, looking truculent. I watched them skulk off into the bushes.
- **slack off** (*a*) (*make a cable loose*) Slack off! (*b*) (*tire, slowly stop working*) Don't slack off (now), just as we are getting to the end. 2 (*loosen*) Slack off those ropes. He slacked off the cable.
- **slack up** (*stop working so hard*) It's time to slack up a bit.

- **slice off** (*remove by slicing*) He sliced off several pieces of meat. The machine sliced the ham off evenly.
- **slice up** (*cut up into slices*) She sliced the sausage up. First you should slice up the meat and the onions.
- **slick up** (*a*) (*make slick or shiny*) He slicked up his hair. (*b*) (*improve*) The comedian was told to slick up his act. (*c*) (*smarten up*) This whole house needs slicking up. He slicked up his appearance.
- **slide + particle** 1 (*slide, with direction*) The snow slid down. The ship slid past. The plunger slides in and out easily. It slides up and down without trouble, if oiled properly. 2 He slid the money over to me. They slid the injured man down on a sledge. He slid the gun out (of its holster).
- **slide off** (*leave*) I'd better slide off now.
- **sling + particle** (*throw violently or casually, with direction*) He slung the box out. I asked him to sling the hammer over. She slung it away in disgust. The equipment had been slung aside almost unused.
- **sling out** (*a*) (*evict*) They have been slung out by their landlord. (*b*) (*sack*) His boss heartened to sling him out.
- **sling up** (*a*) (*hang up in or with a sling*) The equipment had been slung up on the wall.
- **slip + particle** 1 (*move gently, quickly and lightly, with direction*) The boat slipped down into the water. She slipped out to meet him. He slipped in unobserved. They slipped away together. I'll sup back and get it. 2 She slipped the ring off. He slipped the message out through the window. He slipped the clutch in She slipped the dress on.
- **slip down** (*a*) (*slide down, accidentally*) He slipped down into the hole The paper slipped down between the seat and the back of the chair.

- **smooth down** (*a*) (*smooth or caress to lie flat*) He smoothed the fur down. She smoothed her hair down. (*b*) I hope he can smooth the whole matter down.
- **smooth out** (*a*) (*smooth until flat*) She smoothed the creases out with an electric iron. (*b*) She is good at smoothing these little problems out. I will try to smooth things out.
- **smuggle in** (*bring in by smuggling, introduce illegally into a place*) The brandy was smuggled in. They smuggled in some food for the prisoners. A lot of opium is smuggled in every year.
- **smuggle out** (*get out by smuggling, take out illegally*) The goods have been smuggled out by sea. They smuggled him out before the police could stop them.
- **snap at** (*speak angrily to*) She snapped at him when he asked her what she was going to do. Don't snap at me like that!
- **snap off** 1 (*break of sharply*) The branch snapped off. 2 (*a*) (*break of sharply*) He snapped the branch off. (*b*) (*shoot, fire*) The sniper snapped off six rapid shots. (*c*) (*take*) He snapped off several frames.
- **snap out** (*say or speak sharply*) He snapped out an angry reply.
- **snap up** (*grab quickly*) He snapped up the offer. If there are any bargains going, she'll snap them up.
- **snarl up** (*mix or tangle up, confuse*) The wool is all snarled up. The traffic gets snarled up very often at that roundabout. *noun* **a snarl-up.**
- **snatch up** (*pick up quickly and/or roughly*) He Snatched up some food and ran. She snatched up the baby before she fled. The soldiers snatched up their rifles and prepared to fire.

- **sneak + particle** 1 (*sneak or move secretively, with direction*) The thief sneaked quietly up. Shadowy figures were sneaking along near the house. I saw someone sneak away. 2 He sneaked the girl away. I expect she'll try to sneak some friend in (to the party). Don't sneak any liquor out!
- **snip off** (*cut off quickly and/or lightly*) She snipped some hair off with a small pair of scissors.
- **snow in** (*surround with snow, and prevent from moving*) The village has been snowed in for a week. We were snowed in for several days.
- **snow under** (*overload*) The firm is snowed under with work. We really are snowed under with new orders.
- **snow up** (*cover completely with snow*) The whole area is snowed up. The convoy was snowed up on the main road. The mountain passes are snowed up.
- **soldier on** (*carry on like a dutiful soldier, keep on working steadily, persevere*) Well, it isn't easy, but we'll soldier on. He'll soldier on whatever happens.
- **sop up** (*take up by soaking*) She sopped the gravy up with bread. They sopped up the water with cloths.
- **sound off** (*a*) (*sound a bugle*) The bugler sounded off. Bugler, sound off! (*b*) *boast*) He keeps sounding off about his exploits in the Far East.
- **sound out** (*test, check the opinions of*) Can you sound your friends Out and see whether they will help? He will sound them out for us.
- **soup up** (*make more powerful*) He has souped the engine up a lot. He drives a souped-up version of this car.
- **space out** (*arrange in regular spaces*) The foresters spaced the seedlings out in rows. Try to space the work out properly.

- **spark off** (*ignite, cause*) His speech seems to have sparked off a real argument. The management's attitude may spark off a series of strikes.
- **speak for** (*represent*) He says he will speak for us at the committee meeting. Have you got anyone to speak for you?
- **speak up** (*speak louder*) The teacher asked the shy little girl to speak up. Would you please speak up, as we can't hear you: Speak up!
- **speed up** 1 (*a*) (*increase in speed, with past participle speeded*) The car speeded up to a hundred kilometers per hour. 2 (*increase in speed, with past participle speeded*) Can you speed things up at all? I asked them to speed the delivery up.
- **spice up** (*a*) (*add spices to*) She hat spiced the soup up. I like spiced-up food. This dish has really been spiced up. (*b*) (*brighten up, enliven*) Some music might spice the party up a bit. Let's spice things up!
- **spill out** 1 (*scatter out, pour out*) The contents of the box spilled out on the floor. Careful the stuff doesn't spill out! 2 She spilled out the contents of the box onto the floor.
- **sponge down** (*clean down with a sponge or by sponging with a cloth*) He sponged himself down rather than have a full bath. She sponged the sick child down and put her to bed.
- **sponge out** (*clean out with a sponge*) She sponged the wound out gently.
- **sponge up** (*clear up with a sponge*) He sponged up the mess on the floor.
- **sponge (up)on** (*seek money from, live parasitically on*) She enjoys sponging upon them. Stop sponging upon us! He sponges shamelessly on his old parents.

- **spoon out** (*a*) (*ladle or serve out with or as though with a spoon*) She spooned out the syrup. (*b*) Stop spooning out second-rate propaganda.
- **spout out** 1 (*come out in spouts or jets*) The water spouted out from the hole. 2 (*a*) (*emit in spouts or jets*) The whale spouted out water. (*b*) They spout out propaganda from that radio station.
- **spout up** (*pour up in spouts or jets*) Lava spouted up from the erupting volcano.
- **spray on** (*put on by spraying*) They sprayed the paint on. Spray on some weed-killer. You spray this hair lacquer on.
- **spray out** 1 (*emerge in a spray or shower*) The water sprayed out of the nozzle of the hosepipe. 2 (*release in a spray or shower*) When he laughed he sprayed out the food in his mouth.
- **spread abroad** (*disseminate, publicise*) He has spread the news abroad that you are leaving. Spread it abroad!
- **spring + particle** (*leap lightly, with direction*) He sprang out at us. The animal sprang quickly away. She sprang back in alarm. The man sprang across-to help me.
- **sprinkle on** (*put on lightly in droplets*) The priest sprinkled the holy water on. Sprinkle the liquid on carefully.
- **sprinkle out** (*flour out lightly in droplets*) She sprinkled some water out. He sprinkled the liquid out carefully.
- **sprint + particle** (*run-very fast, with direction*) The athletes sprinted past. He sprinted in the winner. Several young men sprinted up to meet us.
- **sprout out** (*burst out or grow*) Greenery has sprouted out in the derelict land behind the factory. Hairs sprouted out from his nostrils.
- **sprout up** (*grow up quickly, rampantly*) Grass has sprouted up everywhere. Weeds are sprouting up.

- **spruce up** 1 (*make oneself look better*) He has spruced up for the interview. 2 (*make look better*) He has spruced himself up for the interview. Let me spruce you up a bit
- **spur on** (*a*) (*goad with spurs*) He spurred the animal on to greater effort. The cavalry spurred their horses on. (*b*) (*encourage, exhort*) They spurred him on to greater effort. This success will only serve to spur her on.
- **spurt out** (*come out in spurts or intermittent jets*) The water spurted out when he turned the tap. Blood was spurting out of the wound.
- **stamp out** (*a*) (*produce by a stamping process*) The machine stamps out various patterns on metal. (*b*) (*eradicate, destroy utterly*) We must stamp out this kind of crime. The defenders were stamped out in the last attack.
- **stand about/around** (*stand idly in a particular area*) The unemployed men were just standing about with their hands in their pockets. Don't stand around doing nothing.
- **stand back** (*stand to the rear, keep clear*) The policeman asked the spectators to stand (well) back. Stand back !
- **stand in with** (*be in conspiracy with, be associated with*) He stands in with those people.
- **stand off** (*keep or stay at a distance*) The ships Stood off and waited for orders. The two fleets were standing off from each other. *Idiomatic*: **Stand offish**= haughty snobbish, distant.
- **stand over** 1 (*wait*) The project is to stand over till next year. 2 (*supervise*) He works better when someone is standing over him. I hate having someone standing over me all the time.
- **stand to** (*prepare for action*) He told his men to stand to. Stand to!

- **stand up for** (*defend, extol*) He stands up for women's rights. Always stand up for your principles. Will you stand up for me?
- **stand up to** (*a*) (*resist, face*) The little boy stood up to the big bully. Stand up to them! (*b*) (*resist, survive*) Your report won't stand up to close scrutiny. His position doesn't stand up to detailed examination. Wool stands up to certain treatment better than other fibres.
- **stare out** 1 (*gaze outward*) She stared out over the sea. They were staring out of the window. 2 (*defeat by staring*) He stared the other fellow out. Stop trying to stare me out.
- **staple together** (*fix together by means of a staple or staples*) She stapled the pages together.
- **start back** (*a*) (*start a return journey*) It's late so we'd better start back now. They started back immediately when they got the news. (*b*) (*recoil, move back suddenly*) She started back in fear when she saw them. The noise made him start back.
- **starve out** (*a*) (*starve into leaving a place*) They decided to starve the enemy out. (*b*) (*reduce by hunger*) The refugees look starved out.
- **stash away** (*hide away, conceal*) He is said to have stashed away a lot of money. Where did you stash the loot away?
- **stave in** (*break and/or push in*) The men staved in the door. The sides of the barrel have been staved in.
- **stave off** (*resist, deflect, keep at bay*) This action may help to stave off later disasters of the same kind. It may be too late to stave off trouble.
- **stay away** (*remain elsewhere*) She is deliberately staying away from the meetings. Why don't you stay away if you don't like us?

- **stay behind** (*remain behind*) The pupil stayed behind to ask the teacher a question. He told them to stay behind for a few minutes.
- **stay out** (*a*) (*remain or keep out*) Please stay out till the work is finished. I told him to stay out. Stay out! Get out and stay out! (*b*) (*remain out of the home, office etc*) He usually stays out late on Friday nights. It's unusual for them to stay out so long.
- **stay up** (*a*) (*remain up in position*) Those rafters don't look strong enough to stay up. The temporary roof won't stay up much longer. (*b*) (*remain out of bed*) He stays up late most nights, reading business reports. It's not like you to stay up after midnight.
- **steam + particle** (*move under steam power, with direction*) The ship steamed out of harbour. I watched the liner steam past. The ferry steamed back and forward. The larger ship steamed steadily ahead.
- **steam out** (*remove by steaming*) The technique steams the dirt out (of clothes).
- **steam up** 1 (*become covered in condensation*) The windows have steamed up. 2 (*a*) (*cover in condensation*) This humidity steams all the windows up. (*b*) (*be angry*) He's all steamed up about losing the Contract. Don't get (so) steamed up about it.
- **step + particle** (*step, walk briskly, with, direction*) The horses stepped past proudly. Would you mind stepping in for a moment? He just stepped out for a breath of fresh air. Step aside and make room for us. He stepped back to admire the painting.
- **step aside** (*a*) (*move from a position of authority*) They expect him to step aside and make way for a younger man. 'I'm not ready to step aside yet.
- **step back** (*a*) (*move into an insignificant position*) He doesn't want to step back from the centre of things.

- **step in** (*intervene*) The government may step in and try to settle the dispute. The police are reluctant to step in.
- **step out** (*go very briskly*) Look at them stepping it out!
- **step up** 1 (*be promoted*) He has stepped up into the management of the firm. 2 (*a*) (*increase, in step is or stages*) The factory has stepped up production. The tempo has been stepped up.
- **stick up for** (*defend*) He always sticks up for her. Can't you stick up for yourself sometimes? Don't stick up for him!
- **stink out** (*a*) (*stink completely, fill with a bad smell*) That animal stinks the place out! (*b*) (*force out by causing a stink*) If you take the beast in there, it'll stink everybody out!
- **stink up** (*fill with a stink or terrible smell*) Those rotten eggs have stunk the place up.
- **stop in** (*remain or stay in*) I'll stop in and look after the kids. She usually stops in on Wednesday evenings. Don't 'stop in just for me.
- **stop out** (*remain, or stay out*) When she's angry with me, she stops out for hours. Don't stop out just because he's coming.
- **stop over** (*stay, break a journey*) I expect he'll stop over with us for a day or two: on his way to New York. She usually stops over with him in London *noun* **a stopover**= a break in a Journey
- **store up** (*keep in supply, store as fully as possible*) He has been storing up food for the winter. Squirrels store up nuts.
- **stow away** (*hide, to get a free passage*) He stowed away to Australia. People used to stow away on ships quite a lot. *noun* **a stow away**=a person hiding for a free passage. 2 (*put or store away*) She stowed the money away in a

drawer. He keeps the cash stowed away in an old sock. Stow it away somewhere.
- **straggle + particle** (*walk slowly, some lagging behind others*) Refugees straggled in all day. Remnants of the army straggled back from the battle. Most of the athletes straggled along behind, taking it easy.
- **strap down** (*fix down with straps*) The patient was strapped down to the bed in case he injured himself by moving. Strap the lid down. and then put the box in here.
- **strap in** (*fix in with straps or a strap*) The driver was properly strapped in. Strap yourself in before starting the engine. I don't like being strapped in.
- **strap up** (*a*) (*fix up with straps*) The equipment was strapped up on to the wall. (*b*) (*restrict as fully as possible with straps*) The prisoner was safely strapped up.
- **stream + particle** (*move along in a stream or in large numbers with direction*) Water was streaming in through a hole in the roof. The blood streamed down from the wound in his head. The people streamed past on their way to the square.
- **strengthen up** (*make strong or stronger*) This food will strengthen you up after your illness.
- **stray away** (*a*) (*wander away and get lost*) Several sheep have strayed away. (*b*) The priest was afraid that some of his parishioners would stray away from the paths of virtue.
- **string out** (*a*) (*put out, on strings*) They strung the pieces of paper out to frighten birds away (*b*) (*extend in lines or strings*) The refugees were strung out along the dusty roads for miles.
- **string up** (*a*) (*put up in or with strings*) We strung the onions up. The nets were strung up under the rafters.

(*b*) (*hang by the neck*) The mob strung up several of the men whom they suspected of murder. String them up!
- **strip off** 1 (*take one's clothes off*) He stripped off and dived into the pool. 2 (*a*) (*remove in strips*) He stripped the tape off. They stripped the bandages off. (*b*) (*pull off quickly*) He stripped his shirt off.
- **struggle along** (*a*) (*manage along with a struggle, get along with difficulty*) The wounded man struggled along somehow. (*b*) They struggled along for some years without much money.
- **struggle back** (*return with difficulty*) The soldiers struggled back to their lines despite heavy enemy attacks
- **struggle on** (*continue to struggle*) The partisans struggled on against the invaders even when there seemed little hope. We struggle on somehow, although there isn't much money.
- **strut+ particle** (*walk with stiff pride, with direction*) The cockerel strutted along. A drill sergeant was strutting about on the parade ground.
- **stub out** (*finish by crushing the stub or butt*) He stubbed out his cigarette (in the ash-tray).
- **stuff down** (*push firmly down*) He stuffed the papers. Down into the box.
- **stuff in** (*push firmly in*) He stuffed the papers in (to the drawer).
- **swab down** (*clean down with a swab or mop*) The sailors swabbed the deck down.
- **swab out** (*clean out with a swab of absorbent material*) The nurse swabbed out the wound.
- **swagger + particle** (*walk with bravado, with direction*) The bully swaggered in. They swaggered out, victorious. I saw some soldiers swaggering along.

- **swallow down** (*swallow, unwillingly*) He swallowed the medicine down.
- **swallow up** (*swallow completely*) He is afraid that the ground will open and swallow him up.
- **swan off** (*go off casually, wander off*) He has just swanned off somewhere.
- **sway + particle** (*move from side to side, gently, with direction*) The drunk man swayed about. The trees swayed back and forward in the breeze. The boxer swayed back to avoid the blow.
- **swear by** (*think highly of, value*) He swears by that shop. I always swear by their products.
- **swear in** (*introduce by requiring to: take or swear an oath*) He swore the witness in. The jury was sworn in.
- **swear off** (*avoid*) He swore off doing-it. I wish he would swear off alcohol.
- **sweat out** (*a*) (*remove by sweating*) He wants to sweat the alcohol out of his system. (*b*) (*endure*) They'll just have to sweat it out (until help comes).
- **swell up** (*become bloated*) The bodies of the dead have begun to swell up. The lump on his neck has swollen up considerably.
- **swerve + particle** (*move in various curves, with direction*) The car was swerving about dangerously. He swerved in and out of the traffic. The fast boat swerved round towards the open sea.
- **swig away** (*take drinks continuously*) He keeps swigging away at that bottle of brandy.
- **swill down** (*a*) (*clean down with plenty of water*) They swilled the pigsty down. Swill it down with a hosepipe. (*b*) (*drink down, consume*) He has swilled down vast

quantities of beer. He swilled the bread down with a mug of tea.
- **swill out** (*clean out with plenty of water*) This room is so filthy it needs swilling out. Swill the place out.
- **swim + particle** (*swim, with direction*) The man swam up to the boat. They swam in for a rest and then swam out again. I watched her swimming away. The children were swimming about in the pool.
- **swing + particle** (*move with a swing, with direction*) The tall man swung along steadily. The monkey swung down from the tree. A jet plane swung round and began to dive over the town.
- **swirl + particle** 1 (*move in swirls or eddies, with direction*) The water swirled past at great speed. Muddy water was swirling up from the great hole. Vapour was swirling out of the volcano. Great clouds came swirling in from the sea. 2 She swirled the cream round with a whisk. The typhoon swirled the sea up into a column of water.
- **swish + particle** (*move with a swishing sound, with direction*) The bicycles swished along through the rain. The branches of the tree swished back and forward against the wall. The glider swished down gently towards the field.
- **switch off** 1 (*disconnect by turning a switch off*) The programme on the radio was dull, so she switched off. We'd better switch off now. When the work was finished, they switched off. 2 (*a*) (*disconnect by turning a switch off*) He switched the radio off. Switch the machine off, please. (*b*) (*prevent or stop from talking*) Switch that fellow off!

T

- **track + particle** (*change course across the wind, with direction*) The ship tacked along. It was necessary to tack back across the bay.
- **tack back** (*a*) (*fix back in position with tacks*) He tacked the carpet back. (*b*) (*fix to one side, by means of tacks*) He tacked the material back (out of the way).
- **tack down** (*a*) (*fix down with tacks*) She tacked the carpet down. (*b*) (*sew down with tacking stitches*) She tacked the pleats down.
- **tack on** (*a*) (*us on with a tack or tacks*) He tacked the sheets of paper on as carefully as possible. (*b*) They tacked the information on at the end of the report. (*c*) (*sew on with tacking stitches*) She tacked the pockets on.
- **tag along** (*come along as a follower*) Oh, I'll just tag along and watch you all playing. She always tags along with them.
- **tag around with** (*accompany*) She tags around with him quite a lot.
- **tag on** (*follow*) He tagged on behind. Stop tagging on to us all the time.
- **tag together** (*a*) (*join together*) Tag these documents together, please. (*b*) I wouldn't tag those events together.
- **tail away** (*diminish*) The numbers in the procession began to tail away. Attendances tailed away towards the end of the course.
- **tail off** (*diminish, lessen*) My enthusiasm has rather tailed off.
- **take + particle** (*take, with direction*) He took the children out. She took the lost cat in. The guards took the

prisoners away. The porter took us up to our room. She took along all the documents she needed. They took me aside and broke the news.
- **take aback** (*surprised*) I was quite taken aback by his attitude. Don't be taken aback by anything she says.
- **take after** (*resemble*) The baby really takes after his father.
- **take apart** (*a*) (*separate from a main group*) He took his disciples apart and spoke with them. (*b*) (*dismantle*) The mechanics took the engine apart. (*c*) (*dismember, murder*) I'll take him apart if I lay my hands on him!
- **take away** (*detract*) This kind of action takes away from his reputation. 2 (*a*) (*subtract*) Take away 2 from 4 and you get 2 (*b*) (*remove*) Take the knife away from that child before he cuts himself. They took away his freedom. These books are not to be taken away. The guards took the prisoner away to jail.
- **take back** (*a*) (*return*) He took the book back. (*b*) (*retract*) He decided to take his threats back. I shall take back my remarks if he will do the same. (*c*) (*agree to receive back again*) She won't take her husband back now, even if he begs her. The grocer took back the rancid butter. (*d*) (*remind of earlier times*) These photographs really take me back (to my youth).
- **take down** (*a*) (*dismantle*) The workmen are now taking down the scaffolding round the building. (*b*) (*write down*) His secretary took down all the points he made. (*c*) (*humble, humiliate*) They want to take him down a bit. **take over** 1 (*accept duty*) I took over from him at six o'clock. The second shift has now taken over. 2 (*a*) (*absorb*) The bigger firm has taken over the smaller one. *noun* **a takeover** *noun* **a takeover bid**= an attempt at a takeover. (*b*) (*assume responsibility for*) He took over

the station last week. I'll take the children over now. He took the business over from his father. He has decided to take over her debts. The new doctor has taken over the duties of the old one.

- **take up with** (*become friends with*) He has taken up with the older boys round the corner. I'm afraid she has taken up with bad company.
- **talk away** (*talk continuously*) She talks away for hours without stopping. 2 (*force to go away by talking*) I'm afraid you won't talk this problem away. He can't talk away his enormous debts.
- **talk back** (*reply insolently*) Don't talk back like that! It is appalling the way that child talks back to his parents.
- **talk down** (*a*) (*reduce to silence by talking*) He is an expert at talking the opposition down. (*b*) (*bring safely down by continuous instructions*) They talked the pilot down to a perfect landing, despite the fog.
- **talk down to** (*patronise*) She talks down to everyone, hut particularly young people.
- **talk out** (*a*) (*discuss fully*) We really ought to talk this matter out sometime soon. (*b*) (*prevent from becoming legislation by spending all the parliamentary time talking*) They have succeeded in talking out that piece of reform.
- **talk over** (*discuss in detail*) We must talk that matter over. It's best to talk these things over quietly.
- **talk to** (*reprimand*) He talked to them very sharply. She needs to be talked to.
- **tally up** (*count up, assess*) The clerks tallied up the number It is difficult to tally up the exact amount of damage suffered.
- **tamp down** (*press firmly down*) He tamped down the tobacco in his pipe.

- **tangle up** (*tangle completely, mix, confuse*) The wires are all tangled up. The dog has tangled up my wool.
- **tank up** (*a*) (*refuel*) We tanked up at the next petrol station. (*b*) (*drunk*) He's completely tanked up.
- **tap back** 1 (*tap in return*) We tapped on the wall and the people on the other side tapped back. 2 (*fix back into place by tapping*) He tapped the nail back.
- **tap down** (*fix down by tapping*) She tapped the edges of the rug down with her heel.
- **tap in** (*fix in by tapping*) He tapped the nails in.
- **tap out** (*a*) (*knock out by tapping*) She tapped the tablets out of the packet on to the table. He tapped out his pipe on the fireplace. (*b*) (*send by tapping*) The operator tapped out the morse signals.
- **tape down** (*fix down with tape*) The carpet is firmly taped down.
- **tape on** (*fix on with tape*) She taped the extra material on.
- **tape together** (*join together with tape*) The two pieces had been taped together.
- **tape up** (*tape as firmly as possible*) He taped up the split in the boards. The kidnappers had taped up their victim's mouth.
- **taper off** 1 (*decrease steadily in size*) The sides of the plane taper off beautifully. Casualties are now tapering off. 2 The carpenter tapered off the edges.
- **tart up** (*a*) (*make oneself like a tart, make up heavily*) She has tarted herself up for her new boy-friend's benefit. (*b*) (*brighten*) Let's tart the design up a bit and surprise everybody.
- **tax away** (*reduce by taxing*) His income is being taxed away. The government seem intent on taxing everything away.

- **team up** (*a*) (*co-operate*) They have teamed up for the project. He has teamed tip with an odd bunch of people. (*b*) (*match, harmonise*) These colours don't team up. 2 (*bring together as a team or into harmony*) He has teamed them up in the hope of getting some good results. It is hard to team these colours up.
- **think back** (*cast the mind back, reminisce*) The photographs made me think back to my schooldays. She thought back and tried to recollect the exact wording of the letter.
- **think out** (*reason out*) I shall have to think this matter out to the end. *Idiom*: Well thought out =well planned
- **think over** (*consider carefully*) I hope you will think matters over before doing anything hasty. Please think it over and let me know.
- **think up** (*invent*) He has thought up some astonishingly original schemes. Whatever will you think up next?
- **thrash + particle** (*move with violent lashing actions, with direction*) The dying fish thrashed about on the beach. The combine harvester thrashed past, cutting and binding the wheat.
- **thrash out** (*a*) (*beat out violently*) I shall thrash the truth out of that boy. (*b*) (*discuss as fully as possible*) The two sides came together to thrash the matter out once and for all.
- **thread in** (*a*) (*introduce as or like a thread*) The machine threads the fibres in. (*b*) The crowd was thick, and he had to thread his way in carefully.
- **throw + particle** (*throw, with direction*) She threw the paper away. He threw the ball up. They threw the books down. He asked them to throw the ball back. The boys were throwing a ball about.

- **throw about** (*a*) (*waste, dispense liberally*) He likes throwing his money about. (*b*) *Idiom*: To throw one's weight about= to use one's strength or power to bully someone.
- **throw away** (*a*) (*waste, thoughtlessly*) You are throwing away your chance of becoming a success. She is simply throwing herself away on a person like that. (*b*) (*say casually*) He threw away a line with great effect.
- **throw down** (*a*) (*surrender*) The men threw down their weapons. The general expected the enemy to throw down their arms soon. (*b*) *Idiom*: To throw down the gauntlet=to issue a challenge.
- **throw off** (*a*) (*escape*) The men threw off their pursuers. (*b*) (*get rid of*) The downtrodden people have at last thrown off the yoke of imperialism. He has thrown off his old habits.
- **throw on** (put on hurriedly) She just threw her clothes on.
- **throw over** (*a*) (*reject, give up*) She has thrown him over for someone else. They have thrown that plan over.
- **throw together** (*a*) (*bring together in close contact for some length of time*) The emergency situation has thrown them together again. It was funny to be thrown together in that way after such a long separation. (*b*) (*assemble hastily*) They have simply thrown that machine together.
- **throw up** (*vomit*) He threw up violently 2 (*a*) (*resign from, eject*) He has thrown up a perfectly good job and gone off somewhere. She threw up every opportunity they ever offered her. (*b*) *Idiom*: To throw up one's hands in despair= to despair completely.
- **thrust + particle** (*push with some force, with direction*) They thrust me aside and went in. The guards thrust

him in and closed the door. He thrust a paper out of the window. She thrust the letter down into her bag.

- **tidy out** (*clean or clear out, in order to make tidy or meat*) She decided to tidy out the upstairs rooms. He tidied out his drawers arid letter, trays.
- **tidy up** 1 (*clear up tidily*) She asked the children to tidy up. 2 (*a*) She tidied up the room. (*b*) (*have a wash, comb one's hair etc*) I'll just run upstairs and tidy myself up.
- **tie off** (*seal off by tying or knotting*) The midwife cut and tied off the baby's umbilical cord. The men tied off the loose ends of the ropes.
- **tie together** 1 (*match*) Their stories don't appear to tie together. 2 (*a*) (*link by tying*) He tied the ends of the ropes together. (b) (Fig) You'll have difficulty tying those loose ends together. He never did manage to tie the bits of the story together.
- **tighten up** 1 (*become tight or more strict*) We shall have to tighten up on security in this department. 2 (*make tight*) He tightened up the screws. The government has tightened up the regulations considerably since last year.
- **tilt + particle** (*move by tilting or toppling, with direction*) The workmen tilted the huge box back. He tilted the frame forward in an effort to move it. They tilted the cabinet over, to see what was behind it.
- **tinker about/around** (*flay or work amateurishly*) He likes tinkering about with watches. He is always tinkering around with his motorbike.
- **tiptoe + particle** (*move on tiptoe, with direction*) The children tiptoed about upstairs. She tiptoed down to see who had come in. The eavesdropper tiptoed quietly away.
- **tire out** (*exhaust, tire completely*) The children have really tired me out today. She's tired out, poor soul. I'm quite tired out.

- **toddle + particle** (*walk like a small child, with direction*) The little boy toddled up to us. (Fern) Well, I'll toddle off now. They toddled away and left us to do the washing-up.
- **tog up** 1 (*dress up*) They togged up and went out. 2 He togged himself up and went out.
- **toll + particle** (*move labouriously, with direction*) The column of wounded soldiers toiled along. He toiled up wearily to the gates of the monastery. She toiled back to the town, half-dead with fatigue.
- **toil away** (*work very hard*) The men have been toiling away all day. She has toiled away at that machine for too long.
- **toil on** (*work on labouriously*) The labourers toiled on to complete the work. We must just toil on and hope for better days.
- **tone in** (*harmonize*) The various notes toned in. This colour tones in nicely with the general decor.
- **tone up** (*improve in health*) These exercises certainly tone you up.
- **tool up** (*prepare the necessary tools*) The factory is beginning to tool up for the new models. Every time there is a change in design, we have to tool up again.
- **top up** (*add in order to make full*) I'll just top up the water level in the car battery.
- **touch up** (*improve, by touches of paint*) He has touched the car up quite a lot.
- **touch (up)on** (*mention briefly*) I feel we should just touch upon some of these interesting points. He only touched on the matter for a few minutes.
- **tour about/around** (*travel about as part of a tour*) The visitors have been touring about.
- **tousle up** (*rumple or disturb*) His father affectionately tousled up his hair. She had a rather tousled-up look, as though she had just got out of bed.

- **tout about/around** (*try to sell anywhere*) He has been touting that stuff about for weeks. Stop touting your wares about.
- **tow + particle** (*pull with a tow-rope, with direction*) The tug towed the big ship in. They towed the boat out. A lorry came and towed the car away.
- **towel down** (*dry down with a towel*) He towelled himself down.
- **trace out** (*a*) (*mark out gently or lightly*) She traced out the shapes carefully. (*b*) (*delineate*) They traced out the design in the sand.
- **track back** (*go back the same way*) They tracked back to their base camp.
- **track down** (*find by hunting*) The police have tracked down the escaped convict. We must try to track these people down. They hope to track down the source of the infection.
- **train up** (*train as fully as possible, educate*) We must train up a new generation of teachers. They want to train up capable people as quickly as possible.
- **traipse + particle** (*move gaily or thoughtlessly, with direction*) She enjoys traipsing about. They all traipsed along to the party. They have traipsed off somewhere.
- **tramp down** (*press down with the foot*) He tramped the earth down.
- **tramp in** (*press in with the foot*) He tramped the stones in.
- **trample down** (*tread down violently or with an effort*) The cows got in and trampled down the standing wheat.
- **trample in** (*tread in violently or with an effort*) All the flowers and fruit canes have been trampled in.
- **transfer + particle** (move, with detection) His offices have been transferred up to the fourth floor. She has been transferred across to the other department.

- **travel + particle** (*travel, with direction*) The gypsies just travel along as they please. He travelled up to Iceland. They slowly travelled down towards the coast.
- **treasure up** (*prize, cherish*) He has treasured up a large collection of valuable coins. I shall treasure up these memories.
- **treat of** (*discuss, cover*) This book treats of Napoleonic history.
- **trick out** (*deck, decorate, clothe*) Her mother has tricked her out in a very gay costume. They have tricked themselves out as sailors for the fancy dress party. The boat has been tricked out very brightly.
- **trickle + particle** (*flow or move in small slow streams, with direction*) The water has trickled away. The stream trickles down into that hollow. Water is trickling out of the bath.
- **turf out** (*eject, expel*) They have decided to turf these people out. He was turfed out (of the club) because he did not pay his debts.
- **turf over** (*cover over with turf*) We intend to turf this space over.
- **turn away** (*a*) (*reject*) They have turned several people way because they have no more accommodation. It is unfortunate that we have to turn these beggars away.
- **turn in** 1 (*go to bed*) We usually turn in about midnight. 2 (*a*) (*hand over to the police*) Please, don't turn me in! (*b*) (*stop*) Oh, turn it in, will you!
- **turn off** (*a*) (*seal, stop*) She turned the tap off. They turned off the water supply. Turn off the gas, please. (*b*) (*stop*) They have turned off the supply of arms and ammunition. (*c*) (*cause to lose interest*) This kind of treatment really turns me off.

- **twitter away** (*a*) (*twitter continuously, keep making small noises*) The birds were happily twittering away. (*b*) She twittered away about her family and friends.

U

- **urge + particle** (*encourage to move or do, with direction*) They urged the horses on with whips. The guide urged the tourists out of the cathedral and into the shops.
- **use out** (*a*) (*use until finished*) I intend to use this jacket out before I buy another one. (*b*) (*exhausted*) The resources of the area are used out.
- **use up** (*use completely, consume*) I expect to use up quite a lot of paper during the next few months. The supply of coal has been used up, and we need more.
- **usher + particle** (*guide or escort, with direction*) We were ushered in by a polite orderly. The guards ushered the visitors out when the ceremony was over.

V

- **vamp up** (*a*) (*concoct, invent*) He vamped up some ugly stories about them. (*b*) (*improvise*) They vamped up the music.
- **vanish away** (*vanish or disappear completely*) The colour just vanished away. The men appear to have vanished away.
- **vault + particle** (*move in a single leap, with direction*) He vaulted over into the garden and ran to meet her. He looked at the fence, then ran to it and vaulted across.
- **veer + particle** (*move rapidly in a curve, with direction*) The little yacht suddenly veered away, caught by a gust of wind. The car veered off to the left.

- **venture + particle** (*move tentatively or adventurously, with direction*) She hasn't dared to venture out since the riots. The hero ventured in, in search of the monster. The men ventured forth to meet the new danger.
- **verge (up)on** (*come close to*) This action verges upon aggression. I'm afraid that his behaviour verges on madness.
- **visit with** (*Visit*) We hope you will visit with us sometime. He went out to visit with some friends.
- **vomit up** (*spew up, regurgitate*) He was so sick he vomited up everything he had eaten.
- **vote down** (*defeat by voting against*) The people have voted him down. Parliament voted down the proposals.
- **vote in** (*elect by vote*) The people have voted in a new government. They voted him in as president.
- **vote out** (*reject through voting*) The people have voted out the old government. They voted him out by a majority of 15.
- **vote through** (*pass by voting*) The assembly has voted the new reforms through.
- **vouch for** (*provide attestation for, guarantee*) I can vouch for his integrity. He asked me to vouch for him, so that he could get the job. I wouldn't like to vouch for the truth of his story.
- **voyage + particle** (*travel for a long time, usually by sea, with direction*) The ship voyaged on into unknown seas. The explorers voyaged down the coast to West Africa.

W

- **wad up** (*form into a wad or pad*) He wadded up the paper into a ball. She wadded up her handkerchief nervously.
- **waddle + particle** (*walk like a duck, with direction*) The ducks waddled up. The rotund gentleman waddled over

and introduced himself. They waddled about, looking at the sights.

- **wade + particle** (*walk in shallow water, with direction*) The men waded about in the stream. He waded in as we waded out. He waded back to the riverbank.
- **wade in** (*join in a fight*) The soldiers and sailors waded in.
- **wade through** (*work steadily and slowly through*) He waded through a lot of work last night. This is a lot to wade through.
- **waft + particle** 1 (*move gently on the wind, with direction*) The scents wafted past. A beautiful odour wafted up from below. A delicious smell wafted out from the kitchen. 2 (*carry gently, with direction*) The wind wafted the boat along. The breeze wafted the scents back to us.
- **wag about/around** 1 (*shake about*) The long poles were wagging about in the breeze. 2 (*wave about in an unsteady manner*) The children were wagging flags about.
- **wait about/around** (*wait rather aimlessly*) They waited about for another bus, but none came. The people seemed to be waiting about for something to happen.
- **wait behind** (*remain behind*) She said she would wait behind for them.
- **wait in** (*stay in a place*) She will wait in till you telephone.
- **wait on** 1 (*remain waiting*) They waited on at the scene of the accident until an ambulance arrived. 2 (*serve at a meat*) He waited on us at dinner.
- **wait out** 1 (*remain outside*) Please don't wait' out in the rain. 2 (*defeat by waiting*) We shall wait the enemy out, and watch them starve.
- **wait up** (*remain out of bed*) I'll wait up till midnight. Please don't wait up for me.

- **walk off** (*reduce by energetic walking*) We tried to walk off the effects of the heavy meal.
- **walk off with** (*a*) (*steal*) He walked off with several watches. (*b*) (*win easily*) She walked off with all the prizes. (*c*) Don't walk off with the idea that (I like them) = don't assume so easily that (I like them).
- **walk on** (*a*) (*continue to walk*) The man walked on until nightfall. (*b*) (*enter the play*) The leading actor now walked on. noun **a walking-on part** (in a play).
- **wallop + particle** (*move quickly but heavily, with direction*) The old truck walloped along. The car was walloping about dangerously. 2 (*strike violently, with direction*) The cricketer walloped the ball away to the boundary. He walloped it out.
- **wallow about/around** (*wade about heavily*) The hippopotamus wallowed about in the mud. They love wallowing about in the baths.
- **wander + particle** (*wander, roam with direction*) The tribe wandered off into the hills. The boys wandered away among the trees. She wandered in, looking rather lost. Some refugees are still wandering about in the area.
- **wangle + particle** (*contrive, with direction*) I'm sure you can wangle the information out of him. He wangled the visitors in for a whole hour. They said they would wangle the business through to a successful conclusion.
- **warble away** (*warble or sing continuously, of birds*) The thrush warbled away on a branch.
- **warble out** (*a*) (*sing out*) The birds warbled out happily. (*b*) (*shout out*) She warbled out something about having a party.
- **ward off** (*a*) (*deflect*) He warded off the blow with a raised arm. (*b*) The general warded off the enemy attack as best we could. This amulet is said to ward off evil spirits.

- **warm up** 1 (*a*) (*get or become warm*) The food has warmed up. (*b*) (*become livelier*) The party has begun to warm up. 2 (*a*) (*heat*) She warmed up the food. (*b*) (*enliven*) They warmed up the party. (*c*) (*re-heat*) She warmed up the leftovers of Last night's dinner. (*d*) (*refurbish*) They have just warmed up the same old plan. It's a warmed-up Version of the old scheme.
- **warn off** (*threaten; tell to keep away*) When we tried to enter the place, some men warned us off. He warns everybody oil who tries to be friendly with his girl-friend.
- **wave + particle** (*cause to move by waving, with direction*) He waved the waiter away. She waved us over to meet her friends. She waved the children out (of the house).
- **wear away** 1 (*a*) (*erode*) The inscriptions on the stones have worn away. (*b*) My patience has worn away. 2 (*a*) (*reduce by rubbing, erode*) Water has worn the banks away. The steps have been worn away by many feet. (*b*) My patience has long since been worn away.
- **wear down** 1 (*erode*) The stone has worn down. 2 (*rub down or erode*) Wind and rain have worn the monument down. (*b*) Inaction has worn down his resolution. His strength has been worn down by illness. (*c*) (*reduce by attrition*) The general has decided to wear down the enemy's strength by a long slow campaign.
- **wear off** (*lose power*) The effects of the medicine have worn off. The novelty has worn off (= something new has lost its special attraction).
- **wear on** (*a*) (*pass*) The day wore on. Time wore on. (*b*) (*continue*) The discussion wore on interminably. The battle wore on through the night.
- **weigh in** (*a*) (*be weighed as part of the preparation for a fight*) The boxers weighed in. (*b*) (*join in vigorously*) He weighed in with a strong argument against the policy.

- **weigh out** (*measure out by weight*) He weighed out three kilos of sugar.
- **weight down** (*hold down with a weight*) They weighted the canvas down with bricks.
- **welcome back** (*welcome home, or back to a particular place*) Although he had left in anger, we all welcomed him back. The travellers were welcomed back with joy by their fellow villagers.
- **welcome in** (*give hospitality to*) The farmer welcomed the people in.
- **well out** (*rise and flow out*) Water was welling out of the ground. Blood began to well out (of the wound).
- **well up** (*flow up*) Oil welled up out of the ground. Tears welled up in her eyes. The floodwaters welled up menacingly.
- **wet through** (*wet completely*) The rain has wet us through. He's wet through.
- **wheedle out** (*obtain by wheedling or teasing*) She wheedled the information out of him. You won't wheedle any more money out of me.
- **wheel + particle** (*move on wheels, with direction*) The men wheeled the aeroplane out. The patient was wheeled in and the surgeon prepared to operate. They wheeled the food away on a trolley. The crippled man wheeled himself along.
- **whisk + particle** (*move or lift lightly, with direction*) A light breeze whisked the papers away. He whisked us off to see the play. We were whisked out to sea ma fast launch.
- **whistle + particle** (*move or summon by whistling, with direction*) He whistled up the dogs. The policeman whistled his colleagues over to see what he had found.
- **whistle up** (*a*) (*make quickly*) She whistled up an excellent snack for us all. (*b*) (*summon quickly*) The

general whistled up reinforcements. He tried to whistle up some help.
- **whittle away** (*reduce gradually by cutting*) He whittled the wood away. (*b*) They are slowly whittling away our power.
- **whizz + particle** (*move quickly, with direction*) The fast car just whizzed along. He whizzed past on his new motorbike. The aeroplanes whizzed away The boys whizzed out to play.
- **whoop up** (*have parties, get drunk etc.*) They enjoy whooping it up.
- **whoosh + particle** (*move with a whooshing or rushing noise, with direction*) The train whooshed past. The waves came whooshing up to where we stood. The churning waters whooshed in and out.
- **widen out** 1 (*become wide*) The peninsula widens out at this point. 2 (*intensive of widen*) They have widened out the shop. The design has been considerably widened out. The general wants to widen out the campaign.
- **wiggle + particle** (*move with wriggling actions, with direction*) The worms were wiggling about. She wiggled up to us.
- **will away** (*give away in a will and testament*) He has willed away the whole estate to strangers. She willed the money away to a home for dogs and cats.
- **win back** (*regain*) He has won back their favour. She has managed to win him back. The team has won back the trophy.
- **win out** (*win in the end, finally triumph*) Good will win out. They will win out in the long run.
- **win over** (*convert, bring over to one's own side*) They have won over a number of opponents. He wins over souls for God. She has won him over completely.

- **win through** (*survive, reach the end successfully*) The candidates all won through. The soldiers have won through.
- **work out at** (*amount to*) The bill works out at Rs 20 each. What does that work out at?
- **write out** (*a*) (*write in full*) He wrote out his notes. The teacher asked her to write the whole thing out. (*b*) (*prepare in writing*) The doctor wrote out a prescription for the medicine. He wrote out a testimonial for me. She wrote out a cheque for Rs 5000.
- **write up** (*a*) (*write as fully as possible*) He wrote up his notes. She wrote up the story of the young lovers. He wrote up his diary. (*b*) (*describe, review*) He wrote the play up in the next edition of the paper. *noun* **a write-up**. *noun* **a bad write-up** = a bad review.
- **writhe + particle** (*move with thrashing actions, with direction*) The injured snake writhed along. The poisoned cat writhed about on the floor.

Y

- **yank + particle** (*pull violently or with a sudden effort, with direction*) The dentist yanked his tooth out. The men yanked him in from the street. The police yanked the offenders off to the police station.
- **yap away** (*a*) (*yap or bark continuously in snappish manner*) The little dog yapped away at us though the fence. (*b*) She was yapping away about her new clothes.
- **yarn away** (*yarn or tell stories continuously*) The men yarned away happily in the bar of the hotel.
- **yell out** 1 (*shout loudly*) The man yelled out in pain. 2 (*shout loudly*) The captain yelled out his commands.

- **yield up** (*yield or surrender completely*) They have yielded up the bulk of their supplies to the enemy.
- **yoke together** (*a*) (*put together under the same yoke*) The oxen were yoked together. (*b*) We didn't expect to be yoked together in the same office.
- **yoke up** (*put into harness or under a yoke*) The oxen were yoked up.

Z

- **zero in** (*come in on the centre or zero of a target*) The bombers zeroed in (on the enemy positions).
- **zip + particle** (*move very quickly, with direction*) The little car zipped along. When the gates opened they zipped through. The little boy zipped out when the door was left open.
- **zip on** 1 (*fit into place with a zip fastener*) The dress zips on. 2 (*fit on by pulling a zip fastener*) She zipped the dress on.
- **zip up** 1 (*close with a zip fastener*) The dress zips up. 2 (*fit into portion by pulling up a zip fastener*) She zipped up her dress.
- **zoom + particle** (*move in a long sweep, with direction*) The aeroplane zoomed down. The sports car was zooming along beautifully. They zoomed off in their new car. The TV camera zoomed in for a close-up of the lovers.